JAMES C. SCHAAP

TAKE IT
FROM A
WISE
GUY

DEVOTIONS ▾ FOR
TODAY'S
FAMILY

CRCPUBLICATIONS
Grand Rapids, Michigan

Illustrated by Paul Stoub

Schaap, James C., 1948-
Take it from a wise guy / James C. Schaap.
p.   cm.—(Devotions for today's family)
ISBN 0-930265-99-8 $5.95
1. Bible. O.T. Proverbs—Devotional literature.
2. Family-Prayer-books and devotions—English.   I. Series.
BS1465.4.S22   1990
249—dc20   90-25406
CIP

ISBN 0-930265-99-8

5 4 3 2 1

CONTENTS

PREFACE

Devotions are defined as "acts of prayer or private worship." Family devotions are those regular times the family pauses—often before or after meals—to read and think about a Bible passage and to thank God for his good gifts.

Given the hectic pace of modern life, "today's family" may have difficulty finding time for such devotions. But it's important that we do so. For the sake of the family's stability and health, such times of united worship are vital.

This little book is offered as a guide for such devotional times. Written in a clear, lively way, it talks directly to families with teenagers. It uses their language. It speaks to their life experiences. It builds bridges between our modern living and the biblical wisdom, written so many millennia ago.

With its collection of fragmentary sayings and pithy admonitions, the book of Proverbs is usually difficult to use for devotions. *Take It From a Wise Guy*, however, makes such use possible, helping families understand and appreciate the profound world-view of this Bible book's wisdom writers.

Life is a battleground between two forces, a contest between two life directions—wisdom and folly, good and evil, the way of life and the way of death. Choose wisdom and life, says Proverbs. This is the way approved by God—the way of health and well-being. The wise person lives in harmony with God's order.

James C. Schaap, author of *Take It From a Wise Guy*, is a professor of English at Dordt College in Sioux Center, Iowa. Prolific writer of short stories and authentic commentator on the Christian community (as seen in a Reformed, midwestern context), Schaap is above all a person who thinks deeply and writes wisely about his own faith experience. His published works include *CRC Family Portrait*, stories about ordinary Christians; *Intermission*, a popular book of devotionals for teenagers; *Someone's Singing, Lord* and *No Kidding, God*, other books in the present series.

Take It From a Wise Guy is offered with the prayer that it may help your family to find and follow the way of wisdom, the way of the "fear of the Lord."

Harvey A. Smit
Editor in Chief
Education Department
CRC Publications

MEETING WISDOM

What is wisdom? That's the primary question, the one this first set of meditations tries to answer.

Wisdom can be many things—listening to parents, staying away from those things that God hates, avoiding life's poisoned pills (the things that look good on the outside but are death to swallow), not playing the fool.

But at its heart, wisdom is seeing clearly. To look at our world and see God's creation; to look at ourselves and others and see God's creatures—that's the beginning of wisdom.

SEEING CLEARLY

....
Proverbs 1:1-7

I remember Melvin from the days I worked as a park ranger. He was the guy who wore binoculars to the beach. Often as not, he scuffed through the dry sand in tennies and argyle socks. His plaid shorts were baggy all right, but not billowy enough to hide the bulky thighs beneath them. Once he got his blanket spread, Melvin would loaf around in his jockey undershirt, the kind with the thin straps. Everybody on the beach would have been happier if he'd kept on his shirt—even if it was the green one with the flamingos.

But Melvin wasn't dumb. He used his binocs with real skill. A calm Lake Michigan is a full gallery of ships, from skiffs to coal barges, and most people thought Melvin brought his binoculars to watch the boats. But we'd seen him operate. We knew better.

A double-masted sailboat could be lolling gently in the rolls a half-mile out or some humongous barge could loom on the horizon, shimmering in the heat waves of mid-afternoon, and Melvin wouldn't even see them. He'd be looking where he always looked—straight down the beach. Because Melvin wasn't after barges. He was after bikinis. While every other guy—including rangers—dared sneak only sideways glances, Melvin sat in the sand and took aim at whatever graceful lines his lenses brought into view.

Melvin's binoculars did what glasses or contacts are meant to do— help us see better by making everything clear. Binocs bring into view what seems afar off. Microscopes offer us a glimpse of worlds we'd never see on our own, even though they exist right around us. And glasses help us read road signs or fine print that could be deadly to miss.

Quite plainly, glasses help us see what we want and need to see. Maybe that's what the French Reformer John Calvin had in mind when he once claimed that the Bible works like glasses on the eyes of the believer: it clears up the darkness, he said, and lets us see God. Everything we see gets bright and vivid and sharp.

The Proverbs act like glasses too. And even though they are thousands of years old, they bring life today into focus. The central truth of Proverbs, summarized here in verse 7, is that "the fear of the LORD the beginning of wisdom." If you want to see clearly, the verse says, then you must know God.

I used to chuckle at what my mother would say every time we saw cattle lounging on some lonesome prairie slope. She probably had never smelled a steer up close, and if she ever made it into a barn, she likely hopscotched out pronto. But every time we'd see beef on some open range, she'd lean back and say, "the cattle on a thousand hills," as if the phrase were sung by a choir.

So today, whenever I see a herd of cows, I still hear my mother's rhapsody—"the cattle on a thousand hills." But today I appreciate what she said, because in that small way she taught me to see even cattle as Christ's. She helped me see that the fear of the Lord *is* the beginning of wisdom.

Proverbs is about seeing clearly and being wise. And it all starts with God. Seeing clearly that God rules this often nutty world is the first step, the book says, to being wise.

....

Thank you, Lord, for appearing in the cattle on a hill,
in the flight of an eagle, in the dance of trees in a
summer wind. Thank you for showing us that this is
your world and help us never to forget that all of
creation rests securely in your hands. Amen.

"FATHER KNOWS BETTER"

....

Proverbs 6:20-23; 23:22-25

When he was little, my son started burping out loud—an early-childhood disease that I think most often afflicts those of the male gender. We told him that such behavior simply wasn't acceptable, at least not in the circles where his parents hang out.

One night I took him along to a softball game, promising that he could sit on our bench and chase bats. Maybe I'm too old to play softball, and maybe I'm slightly overweight, but I still like the game. Every once in awhile I can tag enough of the ball to make me feel as if I'm twenty years younger.

That night I pounded out a double, then scored when the guy behind me punched the ball to right field. I came in gasping, took a chorus of high-fives, and actually believed for a time that I was still twenty-two. I sat down beside my proud son. It was like one of those beer commercials—"things don't get any better than this."

Then, from somewhere deep inside came this tempestuous indiscretion, this walloping belch. "Whhhooommmpp," it went, and right then I remembered everything I'd told my son about indiscreet natural sounds that too easily seep from the secrecy of one's body.

I looked down at David, and he was looking right at me, a lesson from his father's own catechism written in boldface on the wide smile spread across his lips.

The really important idea in today's Scripture is that children should listen to their parents' wisdom. What the passages assume, of course, is that parents have some smarts to pass along. As a father myself, I must admit that these passages make me tremble. The idea of children having to listen to their parents' wisdom is likely as scary for parents as it is sickening to their teenage children. It's up to my wife and me—the belcher—to pass along wisdom to my children. Incredibly formidable.

Sometimes passages like these make you wonder how relevant the Bible is. After all, we're living in a time when belching is the least of sins, when too many fathers beat their kids with belts, when mothers lurch around clutching bottles or crack pipes, when yuppie parents make a habit of hustling off on some exotic cruise to "get away from the kids." Half of our families are broken. We all know a dozen parents who are hip-deep in mid-life crises.

But, if the Bible is to be believed, passing on wisdom is something I *should* do. *Should* is something of a naughty word today. *Should* means guilt; if you don't, you should. *Should* means pressure, restraint, compulsion. *Should* keeps us from finding ourselves. *Should* keeps us in church instead of at the beach. *Should* puts parents on cold metal chairs at the PTA and keeps them out of overstuffed chairs in front of the TV.

One of the important lessons Proverbs teaches my children is that they should listen to my wisdom. In fact, it's more than a lesson—it's a command.

What's more, I should *have* some wisdom that they can listen to. It's an admonition that stings as much on my end as it does on my kids'. Be wise, Dad. And pass on the wisdom.

Dear God, please grant to parents the wisdom they need to help their kids grow into a knowledge of your world. Forgive kids when they don't listen and parents when they don't teach. Help all of us to work at understanding how you would have us live in your world. Help us to love. In Jesus' name, Amen.

HAUGHTY EYES

....
Proverbs 6:16-19

Haughty eyes. The Lord hates haughty eyes.

Let me tell you about haughty eyes. Bobby was in an English class of mine, a class made up mostly of guys who'd just come from an agriculture class. Now the guys in that class didn't go breathless over poetry. They loved the murder and mayhem in Macbeth, but they rolled their eyes something terrible at Shakespeare's love sonnets.

So we're talking poetry one afternoon—wait a minute, *I'm* talking poetry. They're yawning or gabbing or stretching their necks toward the clock over the door. They don't care, so I get mad. I figure the stuff we're studying is interesting. They don't. I yell. You know how that goes.

Bobby is sitting beside a girl with dark hair—someone he's been trying to impress all semester. "Stupid crap anyway," he says.

I let him say it. I figure I'll do better in this class if I let kids speak their minds.

"Listen," I tell him, "what Lowell has to say isn't silly at all. It's about your life."

He smirks, says something out of the corner of his mouth to the kids around him, and they all laugh.

"Bob," I say, "what'd you say? Tell me what you said."

He doesn't say a word. He just looks at me, gives me a pair of "haughty eyes" as if I didn't know diddly.

Immediately I see red. In my hands I can already feel his skinny neck wrung like a wet chamois.

Now Bobby's short and scrawny, a pipsqueak with a complexion so light his nose burns if he gets close to a window on a sunny afternoon. I probably outweigh him by a hundred pounds, and he knows it. So the moment he sees what I'm thinking, he kicks back his stool and takes off running straight out of the room, me behind him.

The thing is, he's quicker—and he knows he's running for his life. He tears down the hallway, makes a left, and flies right out the front door and into the parking lot. For awhile we play this little game, me on one side of a car, him on the other. I go one way, he takes off. Meanwhile, of course, the whole class is back inside, standing at the windows and cheering—for Bobby.

It soon becomes clear that I won't catch him. He smokes and drinks, but he's too quick. So I quit and march right into the principal's office, still puffing. I tell the head man the story and demand that Bobby never set foot in my class again—just because of a look, just because of "haughty eyes."

It's too bad we don't use the word *haughty* much today because it's a good one, a cousin of *height*. Bobby's haughty eyes made me livid because he was "looking down" on what I was up to in class—more importantly, he was "looking down" on me.

The Lord hates haughty eyes, our passage claims. I know the feeling. Who appreciates a sneer?

Me and Bobby? We made up. But he never made it through high school. He went to jail for breaking into a beer truck.

Seven things, the passage claims, the Lord hates. It's not hard to see why. They're all deceitful, arrogant, sinister. They all make us boil. It's wise to avoid what God hates.

Lord, it's easy to sneer. It's easy to lie. It's easy to take advantage of people and to hurt them. And it's really not hard to make up stories about people we dislike. Keep us from sin, Lord, because it comes so easily. Forgive us when we fail. Amen.

FORBIDDEN FRUIT

....
Proverbs 9:1-6; 13-18

Who can really blame Adam and Eve? The Lord puts them into this incredible garden of delights, gives them freedom, lets them run around naked, and blesses them with every joy imaginable. Then he tells them there's this one little, itsy-bitsy catch.

"By the way," he says, "there's just one tree that's off-limits. Stay away, see?—or else you're going to be in big trouble. Take a bite from that fruit, and you're *history*."

So who wouldn't be curious? I don't care if the place had the sweetest plums imaginable, I'd probably be interested in just one little chunk of that forbidden fruit. Just a taste?

* * * * * *

Belinda walks into a store and checks out the new shorts, the bright ones in vivid fluorescents—day-glo orange, stop-sign red, livid lime. She slips on a pair—cotton, soft against her skin—and it fits. In the fitting-room mirror, she sees the way it'll grab attention. It's perfect, she thinks.

She pulls on her jeans and walks out, laying three others on the counter for the saleslady. She hangs around the store for awhile, admiring fashion watches, then walks out casually, buying a candy bar from the rack at the checkout. Outside, the store detective raps Belinda's shoulder and asks her to come with him. She's dead. She's caught. Her heart sinks to the sidewalk. What's she going to say to her parents?

You know something? In her purse, Belinda had the money to pay for the shorts. She simply chose not to.

* * * * * *

In today's passage, wisdom is contrasted with folly—smarts with stupidity. Both are drawn into cartoon-like figures.

Wisdom has her house in order. She does things right, sending out her servants to advertise what she has to offer—a bountiful supper of smarts sure to make her guests wise.

But Stupidity is on the prowl. Ms. Folly sits up above the city and sings the same tune as Ms. Wisdom, but the lyrics aren't quite the same. "Stolen water is sweet," she croons, "and food eaten in secret is delicious." And then she laughs in her own low-pitched, throaty voice. "Nyah hah haaaa. Come vit' me and 've shall make beautiful music togethaa."

"Just this one apple, I don't want you to touch."

"These shorts are just perfect."

"Stolen water is sweet."

You'll miss the whole point of the book of Proverbs if you think Folly is a warthog. If you want to see her in all her charm, dress her in your favorite fantasy. Give her Madonna's sexiest black formal. Imagine her with long, flowing, beautiful hair. Paint her face with a luscious smile, and set her gracefully in the soft leather seats of a Porsche. Then wave her good-bye.

It ain't easy. No sir. No ma'am.

Folly's got looks all right, but wisdom stays around.

Help us to resist temptation, Lord. Open our eyes to see it when it's there in front of us. And help us to know what's right and what's not. Give us wisdom, Lord. Give us your grace. Amen.

CHOICES I

Chad leaned hard on the armrest to get a better look—not up front where the play was, but off to the side, third row, second seat from the left, where he could just see a few loose strands of Nancy's hair falling softly to her shoulder. It reminded him of the way her hair had looked that night he took her to the prom, of her perfect shoulders above the white, strapless gown . . .

Ginny giggled. He'd almost forgotten he was with her.

"A raccoon coat?" she said, as if she didn't believe it. "Oh, Chad, that's really dumb."

He looked at her strangely.

"Aren't you listening?" she said. "He gave her a raccoon coat— she's going to kill him."

Colonel Heath stood at the front of the stage, almost weeping. Behind him, Geraldine held the coat out at arm's length, as if it were laced with skunk musk.

"I don't get it," Chad said.

Ginny waved him off. "I'll tell you later," she said.

Chad figured that even though he and Ginny were such good friends—buddies all through the last semester—she probably didn't know what was going on in his head. She didn't know that when he called her, it wasn't really like a date at all. He just needed somebody for this one night, a stand-in.

He saw the way Nancy tucked her shoulder into Gregg's, so he reached for Ginny's hand.

She seemed shocked. "I didn't know you cared," she said, laughing. "Does this mean we're going together or something?"

"It's against some law to hold a girl's hand?" he said.

"Not now," she told him. "Later, Romeo, all right?"

Chad held on anyway, grabbed her fingers with his, and when he didn't let go, she raised her eyes and smiled. He glanced back at Nancy and imagined it was her hand—Nancy herself beside him.

The crowd roared at some joke, and Ginny leaned back. "Incredible," she said. "She took it! Love conquers all."

Chad had no idea what was happening on stage. Through the cracks between the people seated at the end of the row he could see Nancy raise her fingers to her lips to cover her laugh. He'd told her once there would never be anyone else. He'd said it on the way home from skiing, just the two of them. He'd figured she'd never forget.

The applause rang like an alarm in his ears, and everyone stood. Chad grabbed his program and shoved it in his pocket.

"What a great idea," Ginny told him as she followed him out of the row. "I didn't know you liked plays. This was terrific, Chad. I loved it." She turned up the row and looked for the exit light. That's when she spotted Nancy. She stiffened. "Take me home," she said, pulling her hand out of his. "Take me home right away."

"Imagine that," he said, "there's Nancy. See her?"

"You mean you didn't know?" Ginny asked.

"How could I?" he said. "Just looked like a good play. Besides," he said, "I don't ever want to see her again."

"Really?" she said.

"Honest to God, Ginny," he told her, taking her hand again.

Lying comes so easily to us, Lord. We try so hard to protect ourselves that the truth goes out the window. Forgive us for talking lies. Forgive us for hurting others by not telling the truth. Amen.

WISE WORDS

If wisdom begins with the eyes (clear seeing), it rests on the lips (right talking). "The tongue of the wise commends knowledge, but the mouth of the fool gushes folly" (15:2).

Speech is the key to our social living. Gossip, careless talk, mischievous words, and false witnessing all destroy human relations. Lying can kill; truth can bring life. So the wise person guards the tongue, knowing its power to hurt or to heal.

FOOLS

....
Proverbs 18:20-21; 25:8-15

Blockhead, woodenhead, fathead, pinhead, thick-head, bonehead, beetle-head, dunderhead, blunderhead, muttonhead, cabbage-head, chucklehead, saphead, rattlehead.

There. If you have any trouble with your idiot brother, lay a couple of those on him.

On the other hand, if your sister's driving you up a wall, try these: airhead, bimbo, no-brain, lackbrain, birdbrain, beanbrain, scatterbrain, dirtbrain, dimwit, numbskull.

Every generation has its selection of prime "cuts": today *dweeb*, *geek*, *nerd*, and *sleazeball* are common in many areas. If we take a trip back to the Put-down Museum, we can pick up a few great hall-of-famers: *dip*, *drip*, *ninny*, and *nincompoop*—and that's just for starters. Of course, I'm leaving out a bunch not fit to print. Most of you can add another dozen, maybe more—including a whole herd derived from a biblical word for donkeys.

I'm not proud to admit it, but (nyuc, nyuc, nyuc) I've always been a fan of the Three Stooges. They used to be on for a solid hour on Saturday mornings—three separate episodes, each of them almost twenty minutes long. I'd sit in front of the TV and watch Moe belt Curly and Larry and call them every name in the book. In minutes I'd be on the floor in near-terminal stomach cramps.

Today if I sneak home a video of the Stooges, I often end up watching it alone. My wife thinks they're disgusting, and my daughter doesn't find them particularly funny. But I like them—and so does my son.

Maybe one reason I enjoy the Stooges is that deep down I'd like to call people ugly names and slap them around. I don't, of course, but maybe I like the Three Stooges because they do what I can't. When I watch them, I get the feeling I'm knocking heads myself, calling those knuckleheads the pea-brains they are.

On that score, I don't think I'm the only sinner. If the Proverbs are to be believed, most of us enjoy putting other people down. Few of us use our fists, of course; but just about all of us, at one time or another, use words.

The gist of today's Scripture passages is that words count. They mean something because they do something. Foul-mouthed rap groups and smut-choked comedians may claim that what they do and say doesn't hurt anyone, but Proverbs says that that idea is plain wrong. Words (18:21) have the power of life and death.

How so? Take it from a teacher. Tell a kid he's a moron every day of the semester, and you'll kill him—not physically, of course, but inside something will die. Why should it be any different for a brother or a sister—or a son or a daughter? One of the Billy Goats Gruff used to say that sticks and stones would break his bones, but words would never hurt him. That may be true for billy goats, but what do they know about humans?

And then there's this idea: slap people around with words, Proverbs says, and it simply reflects on you because, after all (4:23), YOU ARE WHAT YOU SAY. Tell you what, if you call somebody a *hairball* today, make a point of staying away from mirrors, okay?

Keep us from thinking we're so great, Lord. And forgive us when we put other people down—no matter why we do it. Help us to see that we are all your children and that we're all made in your image. Give us the strength and will and faith to love as you would have us love. In Jesus' name, Amen.

PRUDENCE AND THE PRUDE

....
Proverbs 12:6, 13-23

Before we go a step further, we should look at a word that comes up frequently in Proverbs but rarely in ordinary speech.

A friend of ours who taught kindergarten for the last thirty years says that when she started teaching it was hard to get five-year-olds to open up. They'd come to school scared silly, always on the brink of tears, most of them homesick.

Not anymore, she said. Today's kindergartner swaggers in with a chaw of bubble gum in his mouth and a Walkman clipped to his suspenders. He bellies up to the teacher's desk and blurts out, "You in charge here—or what?" Then he tells her he'll have a Mellow Yellow before nap time because milk is for kids.

I'm overstating, of course. But our friend claims that today's kids spout off the very moment they get to school.

What all big mouths lack—kindergartners or adults—is prudence. Prudence isn't exactly a hot commodity in a society that prides itself on doing its own thing. "Let it all hang out," people used to say. "If it feels good, do it." Today the phrase is a bit shorter, but the meaning is the same: "Just do it." You can find those words printed in rainbow colors over the chests of hundreds of different t-shirts in stores from the east coast to the west.

Prudence won't let us "just do it." Prudence acts likes brakes on a car—it slows us down. Prudence makes us step back and think things through before acting. A person who exercises prudence, according to Proverbs, is no dummy.

Twice today's Scripture passage uses the word *prudence*, both times when comparing people who have their heads on straight with those who don't: "a fool shows his annoyance at once; but a prudent man overlooks an insult" (v. 16); and "a prudent man keeps his knowledge to himself, but the heart of fools blurts out folly" (v. 23).

Prudence, according to the dictionary, is "showing carefulness and foresight, avoiding rashness." Its roots reach back to the French language and our word *providence*. When we speak of God's providence, we're referring to his wide vision of things, to the fact that he sees past what's blocking our view. When we act with prudence, we look ahead—beyond the immediate.

Now nobody wants to be called a prude. A prude is an old lady with warts on a double chin that's always hung in a frown because she's afraid that someplace people are having more fun than they should. A prude is a snarling man whose only joy in life is saying no. A prude is somebody scared to death of getting his hands dirty.

But a prude has nothing to do with being prudent—even though the words look like kissing cousins. The word *prude* has its roots not in *providence* but in a picture of an overly strict, powerful woman. The words aren't even related.

A prude is uptight; prudence is just being smart. Don't confuse them, or you won't get a thing out of Proverbs.

Prudence is a great virtue. According to our passage today, it's knowing that keeping your trap shut will keep you from stepping into it yourself. Prudence is wisdom.

....
Lord, teach us to number our words. Teach us when
to say things and what to say. Lord, give us wisdom,
and thank you for your grace. Amen.

PRIMARY INVADERS

....

Proverbs 26:18-28

I lost a lot of sweat in the last few weeks digging out all kinds of things from what had become a weed bed on the north side of our house. Three years of drought and a ton of old shingles from last year's roofing job had smothered what was once a soft bed of tall ferns, so we decided to start from scratch.

I dug it all up—volunteer trees, a few old ferns, some really devious sumac, a tangle of something strawberry-looking, webs of creeping jenny, and a hodgepodge of other junk. It took hours to spade that madness into smooth dirt—clean and pure.

A friend of mine whose masters degree officially made him a "weed scientist" told me my newly-cleaned bed would undoubtedly now be a target for "primary invaders," those plants with mobile seeds that just love virgin territory. Every neighborhood has primary invaders, he explained—plants such as dandelions with their white "fluff" and maple trees with their thousands of whirly birds—the first weeds to show up and bury themselves in sweet new soil.

I got to thinking about "primary invaders." Not long ago a flood swarmed through a city near here, filling basements with thick muck, breaking walls, and creating a catastrophic mess. Within hours, the river fell back into its banks, and just like that the next flood arose—a sea of primary invaders who drove into the neighborhood to gawk at the horror, filling the streets so that work crews couldn't get in to do their thing.

Anytime there's a tragedy—a car accident, a fire, a natural disaster such as a flood—we all have the tendency to turn into primary invaders, gawkers, spectators, thrill-seekers. Why? Perhaps because we're always lured, almost mystically, by the big story—especially by horror. I know I am. Last summer United 232 crashed in Sioux City, Iowa. Since then, whenever I fly out of that airport, I find myself looking for scars in the fields where the burning plane came to rest.

Interest in other people's problems is not wrong, of course. Concern is a measure of compassion and caring. But concern is often a hairsbreadth away from gossip. Concern shows itself in aid; gossip is revealed is the hands-on-hips stance of leering spectators.

The passage today indicts the primary invaders of our lives. "The words of a gossip," it says, "are like choice morsels." Of course they are. We eat up the spicy little tidbits of other people's problems. "They go down to man's inmost parts," the verse goes on to say. The words of a gossip linger, stay in our souls like a cancer, or even a parasite, demanding more.

Let's face it, gossip—both the telling of it and the hearing of it—is the stock in trade of small minds. And we're all guilty. No one can throw a stone here. We love to get the goods on an ex-friend, to hear about failure. I dare say adults are worse than kids. But no matter—if the news is juicy enough, we all love to pass it on.

Not smart, says the book of Proverbs.

Weeds were a part of Adam's curse all right, but sin itself is the primary invader of our lives.

"Psst—you hear what happened to the mayor?"

....

Thank you for Christ's example on earth, Lord.
Thank you for showing us how to love. We all fail,
but what Christ did for us gives us hope and a way
to live in a world where hating each other and saying
bad things is sometimes too easy for all of us.
In your name, Amen.

BITE-SIZED SMARTS

....
Proverbs 6:12-15; 30:32-33

The Proverbs were written for people who hang out at malls, play slow-pitch softball, tease their brothers and sisters, love tacos, and hate broccoli. In fact, they were written for everybody.

But the smart people who put them in one thin book a couple of thousand years ago weren't thinking of Nintendo freaks, single mothers, or yuppies. The audience they had in mind was the young princes who spent their lives hanging out around the king's court—the leaders of society in Solomon's day.

If you've seen the *Karate Kid*, you'll remember the old Chinese man who uses chewable pieces of wisdom to explain things to a picked-on kid. "My son," he says, "man with one tooth eats no apples," and the boy nods, lost in thought. Through the old man's teaching the boy learns discipline and self-control, and, at least in the original *Karate Kid*, becomes adept enough to out-muscle the bully.

The wise men who thought up the Proverbs (Solomon wrote some, but so did others) were very much like that old bearded man. And the lessons they wanted to teach the young princes often come in those same little bites of wisdom: "As twisting the nose produces blood, so stirring up anger produces strife."

Words have this odd gunpowder quality: the tighter you pack them, the bigger the explosion. I once asked a class what this proverb meant: "You can't put pink ribbons on wooden shoes." (In case you don't know yourself, don't forget that wooden shoes were not worn for folk festivals but for cleaning the barn!) One kid told me exactly what the proverb means, and he did so by reciting another proverb: "You can't make a silk purse out of a hog's ear," he said. The Proverbs are bite-sized chunks of 100 percent wisdom that stick to your innards.

Now you might wonder why passages like today's are even in the Bible—after all, not one of them even mentions Christ. The passage from chapter 6, for instance, simply says that the guy with shifty eyes who's trying to wreak havoc on the court—a worthless person with a false mouth—will fall on his face. It doesn't say the Lord will cut him down. Sometimes the Proverbs seem to so totally forget about God that they could well have been written by the old man in the *Karate Kid*.

But let's not forget the big picture here. The opening lines of chapter 1 say "The fear of the LORD is the beginning of wisdom"—that's the basic melody for the whole symphony of truth here. Wisdom, the book says, all starts with being in awe of the great I AM, the God of the Universe.

This week's Scripture deals with the problems people run into because of their big mouths. Today's passages talked specifically about using our big mouths to undermine authority, to create grumbling and chaos. You can't have chaos in the king's court or the whole realm suffers.

But the idea for all of us—from Solomon's princes to California's skateboarders—is to watch the mouth because, well, "a fool's lips bring him strife, and his mouth invites a beating (18:6)." Ouch. I couldn't have said it better myself.

....

Thank you for the book of Proverbs, Lord, for all the
wisdom it offers us. Help us to learn from it. Help us
to wear the glasses it gives us to see the world you've
created. Amen.

CHOICES II

Ginny

Some guys are just friends, you know? You never expect to date them—they're just buddies. Nothing else. Good friends.

That's the way it was with Chad. All semester long we sat together in Geometry and went over axioms and theorems and proofs, drawing up little tables to prove how much fruit is in a watermelon if it's this long and this wide. We laughed, like friends do.

When I saw Nancy at the play, I knew right away why Chad had asked me out—and it wasn't because he liked me. Sure, he *likes* me all right—but only as a friend.

So he lied to me. An outright lie. He said Nancy's got nothing to do with it. He's my friend, right—you don't question friends. But, I knew he was lying, just the same.

We were behind Nancy and her date—I think his name is Gregg something. We were walking down the sidewalk in front of school maybe twenty feet behind them.

"What are we going to do?" I said. I was trying to be nice.

"What?" he muttered, as if he wasn't even tuned in.

So I said, "Earth to Chad, earth to Chad," and he scowled at me. "You got something else on your mind, don't you?" I said. "You got her on your mind. Why did you lie to me?"

I wanted to stay his friend. I could understand him taking me out just to have Nancy see him with another girl. But I didn't like to be lied to. Nobody does.

"We're history," Chad said. "Me and that lying dork?—we're history." He snarled—really—as if he were mad. But I knew him too well. And his lying about it just killed me. All I wanted from him was the truth. I wanted to keep him as a friend.

"So why'd you break up?" I asked him when he opened the car door for me, like a real gentleman. "She do it or you?" I slid all the way over to the passenger's side.

Chad acted like he didn't hear the question. He changed the sub-ject. "I could just as well call you on the phone," he said when he saw where I was sitting. "You'll freeze over there."

I wasn't about to let him change the subject. "I asked you why you broke up," I said.

He got in and started the car, then looked all over. I knew he was looking for Gregg's car, waiting for them to pass us.

I could play this game, too, I figured. "They're they go," I said, when I saw Nancy in a big, white, expensive car.

"Who?" he asked.

"Nancy," I told him. "You know, Nancy Grimm—beautiful hair. You used to go with her." It was starting to bug me.

"Ginny," he said, "I told you to forget it. What's with you anyway? You don't want to be with me—is that it? You'd rather go with some-body else?" Now he was mad. "You want out?" he said. "All you do is tell me how much I'm paying attention to her. If you don't want to be with me, then get out."

All I wanted to do was save our friendship. Maybe I should have stepped right out of his car, right then and there, and left him. I would have slept better that night. I would have slept period. And I would have had a lot better memories, too, really.

But I stayed with him, and I'd do it again. I liked Chad.

....

*Dear Lord, when we treat even our friends poorly,
we don't deserve your love and forgiveness. But you
give it to us anyway because your love is greater
than ours. Thank you for the gift of grace. Thank you
for making us your family. Amen.*

THE POWER OF MONEY

To the wise, money is not a symbol but a tool. Money should neither draw a line between two classes of people, the rich and the poor, nor serve as an excuse for looking down on others with contempt. Money is for using wisely and mercifully, not for holding tightly and selfishly.

Why? Because money never lasts: riches can disappear overnight. And wealth is no index of worth: rich and poor are both created by God and live by his grace. So ask God for enough money to live comfortably, nothing more.

MONEY AND POWER

....
Proverbs 6:1-5; 22:7, 26-27

I write this great novel, but nobody will publish it. One day I see an ad that says a place called Advantage Press will publish books for authors, so I write and ask for information. In a few weeks I get this pretty brochure that says they'll print my great novel—but it'll cost ten thousand dollars.

I'm a poor struggling artist. I don't have ten grand, and the likelihood of my getting it is remote—unless, of course, my novel gets published and five hundred million people pick it up off K-Mart counters all over North America.

I'm sure my novel is a blockbuster. It's got this great car chase, a half-dozen steamy bedroom scenes, and the world's most beautiful dachshund—and it's set in Monte Carlo. It's guaranteed stuff. I know Stephen King will love it, and Spielberg will buy up the movie rights. So I go to the bank, tell them about the book, and ask them to lend me the ten grand.

"Who's going to back you up?" the bank guy says.

"What do you mean, 'back me up'?" I say.

"Who do you have to lean on? Can you get somebody else to stand behind you—with the enchiladas?"

"With money?" I say.

"No, with graham crackers," the banker says.

I don't like his sense of humor.

But I've got this friend who goes school-to-school selling fluorescent shoestrings to sixth graders. Makes big dough. So I call her up. "Beaknor," I say, "how's about standing behind me for ten grand. It's a gimme."

"Whatcha' mean?" she says.

"I mean I need somebody with bucks in her pockets to sign on the dotted line. Just be there is all," I say.

Beaknor's my friend. What does she do?

If she's read Proverbs 6, she stammers a little first; if she's read Proverbs 11:15, she just hangs up the phone. "He who puts up security for another will surely suffer, but whoever refuses to strike hands [you can read "shake hands" here] in pledge is safe."

The advice Proverbs gives about money doesn't sound as if it will help anyone win friends or influence people. We live in a world where corporate takeovers are all the rage. You've got to have backers for any kind of leveraged buy-out.

We all borrow, and at least some of us lend. But Proverbs says that if you want to be free, you should keep your money at home. If you want to keep your good name, don't sign your name to back up other people—even if they're your friends. That sounds almost wicked, doesn't it? After all, a friend in need is a friend indeed.

Here we go again with prudent. If you want to keep your friends and your freedom, Proverbs says, be prudent—neither a borrower nor a lender be.

Maybe the best way to understand the prudence suggested here is to look again at 22:7: "The rich rule over the poor, and the borrower is servant to the lender."

Money, that verse says—today or a thousand years ago—is power. Use it wisely. Be prudent with your petty cash.

....

*Lord, thank you for friends. They are a great blessing
in our lives. Help us to know how to be friends, how
to help when we can and stay away when we must.
Help us be the kind of friends you would have us be.
Amen.*

INVESTMENTS

....

Proverbs 14:31; 19:17; 22:9, 16, 22-23

Everybody feels sorry in a *general* way for "poor" and "homeless" people. But sometimes when "the poor" have faces and stories, appreciating them—and helping them—gets much tougher.

* * * * * *

Bruce Folgersten is 39. He's been married twice and now lives alone in an abandoned Olds. Bruce has been in and out of drug rehab three times, twice on court order. He smokes two packs of Luckies a day and hasn't seen his kids in eight years. He says he doesn't care.

Bruce sleeps poorly, has since Vietnam. He keeps a .38 beneath the drivers seat, even though he'd be thrown back in prison if he were found carrying it. He's not worked for awhile.

* * * * * *

Alice Sand is a welfare mother. She has five kids from two different dads, neither of them her husband. She dropped out of high school when she was fifteen to have her first baby, and she never went back.

Alice lost her apartment eight months ago and now gives her mother's address as her home—even though she doesn't live there. Most nights, Alice works the streets. She sees her kids when she gets the chance.

* * * * * *

Fenwick Hannenberg sometimes—just sometimes—thinks clearly. Often as not, he's lost in a dream world.

During the afternoons Fenwick panhandles; in the evenings he eats from the dumpsters behind the restaurants on Shilling Avenue. He's been in an institution, and hated it—demanded out. When you see him on the street, his eyes seem to blaze.

Fenwick sleeps in an elevator shaft in an abandoned building, where he's thumbtacked a picture of Mickey Mouse to the wall. He's started more than a half dozen fires and never once been caught. Sometimes at night he laughs wickedly.

* * * * * *

North America today is well outfitted in safety nets. If a family loses their house to a late-night fire, likely as not insurance will help—as will neighbors, of course. As a result, the really poor in our society today are often people like Bruce and Alice and Fenwick.

It's not easy to love Bruce; he's potentially violent and often drunk. Alice is no sweetheart herself; she sleeps with guys for money. And Fenwick—sometimes it seems he doesn't want anything more than he's got right now. All three of them may well be very hard to love.

In spite of what we might like to believe, there is no proverb that says "The Lord helps those who help themselves." Neither is there a verse anywhere that tells us to avoid helping poor people whom we don't think deserve our help. What the passages today tell us is quite clear: "He who is kind to the poor lends to the Lord."

The whole Bible echoes that same promise: "A generous man will himself be blessed for he shares his food with the poor." If you are generous, if you care, if you give, if you love—you will be rewarded. But it's not a case of tit-for-tat: the Bible doesn't say that if we help the poor, the Lord will drive up in a Rolls and deliver the Publishers' Clearinghouse grand prize.

Wisdom, Proverbs says, lies in being generous. Investing in the poor is investing in God, because the poor are not a burden; they are—warts and all—our opportunity to love God.

It's so easy for us to think we're better than other people or to avoid seeing others as individuals. Give us the patience and the understanding to deal with the problems of our world, Lord. Help us work hard to help where help is needed, to give a hand to those whom no one else loves. Amen.

OZY

Proverbs 22:1-2; 23:4-5; 27:23-27

I met a traveler from an antique land
Who said: Two vast and trunkless legs of stone
Stand in the desert. Near them, on the sand,
Half sunk, a shattered visage lies, whose frown,
And wrinkled lip, and sneer of cold command,
Tell that its sculptor well those passions read
Which yet survive, stamped on these lifeless things,
The hand that mocked them, and the heart that fed:
"My name is Ozymandias, king of kings:
Look on my works, ye Mighty, and despair!"
Nothing beside remains. Round the decay
Of that colossal wreck, boundless and bare
The long and level sands stretch far away.
                                    —Percy Bysshe Shelley

You may have read this poem before; it's very famous, and it's called, quite simply, "Ozymandias." I don't want to be Mr. Literature Teacher here and talk Shelley's poem to death, but I think it fits with the verses you've just read.

The author says he heard this story from an explorer he bumped into, a man whose name he must not have picked up. Apparently, this traveler had been kicking around the desert when he happened to find a withered and weathered monument to a king nobody knows, Ozymandias. It's only by chance the traveler bumped into the monument; it's only by chance the author heard the story; and it's only by chance that we hear it ourselves. It's almost freaky. Old Ozy must have been an important character, but we could have died easily without ever hearing his name.

What makes this story especially strange is that in some long ago time this Ozymandias was king of the hill. He wanted the sculptor who did his famous face to write in the caption: "Look on my works, ye Mighty, [as if he was the mightiest of the mighty] and despair." You can hear a drum roll behind the words. Yet today, this once famous face shows up in the wastes of some desert landscape—like space junk or empty pop cans and fast food wrappers.

The sculptor apparently was no dummy. He must have seen Ozy's pride and ruthlessness as he chiseled the "wrinkled lip" and "sneer" into this great stone face. The traveler says that this much remains anyway—the sculptor's vision of Ozy's world-class arrogance.

But nothing else marks the king's passing—not a museum or a road sign or a historical marker or a tourist trap where the traveler can buy an Ozymandias T-shirt. All that's left is some silly, vainglorious epitaph and Ozy's face with a mouth full of sand.

When Shelley wrote the poem at the turn of the nineteenth century, most Europeans couldn't help but see Ozy as Napoleon, the squat little general who wanted to rule the world. But the poem is not only about Napoleons or Hitlers; it's about all people who spend their lives foolishly gunning for money and power.

What today's Bible passages say probably won't come as news to any of us: "Riches do not endure forever, and a crown is not secure for all generations." Most of us know that it's not wise to spend life dying for riches and power. But that warning needs repeating, time and time again. The Bible says, "The love of money is the root of all evil." It's that simple.

When everything around us begs to be bought, Lord,
help us to know that money isn't everything. The
greatest possession we have is our knowledge that
you love us. We thank you for dying to save us from
our sin, and we ask you to strengthen us to live for
you forever. Amen.

THE BLESSINGS OF DAILY BREAD /OR "IF I WERE A RICH MAN . . ."

....

Proverbs 30:7-9

A woman I once knew divorced her husband after he'd officially been a doctor for only one year. For several years she'd worked night and day, she told me, to get her husband through medical school. She slaved away with her hope focused like a laser on his finishing. He did. But then their marriage died. Money killed it, she said. That first year he made a hundred grand and neither of them could adjust from having nothing to having big bucks.

The very simple and beautiful prayer of the passage today asks the Lord for two blessings: truth and daily bread. According to the note at the beginning of the chapter, the words belong to Agur, son of Jakeh, probably an oracle or wise man, a person gifted to speak truth clearly. We'll hear more of him later.

Rather than preaching, as so many proverb writers do, Agur, in these verses, simply repeats his own prayer. First, he tells God that he hopes to have no part of lying lips—either his own or others. And second, he prays for his daily bread—just enough of life's goods to be happy. Agur knows that poverty can sometimes push us to desperation, to stealing or even worse; on the other hand, he knows that too much money makes us think we can cut it on our own—as if we don't need God. Wealth and poverty, Agur knows, are both dangerous. Therefore, he says (just as Christ says) give me, please, my daily bread—just enough for what I need.

I'm no crypto-communist. What has happened in the world in the last several years, to me, has been thrilling. Freedom won an epic victory with the collapse of the Berlin Wall. But even freedom has its silliness. If the people of Poland, East Germany, or Czechoslovakia become free only to build better theme parks, then they may be richer than they were but they won't be any happier. Freedom, it seems, makes the grass across the block look very well-fertilized.

Agur prays for just enough—not too little or too much. Sometimes it takes a very dramatic lesson to teach us what "just enough" means . . .

Linda would have killed to be store manager. She'd waited on customers with stinky feet since she was sixteen, full-time since she graduated. She had four year's experience when the management slot opened up, and she thought she deserved the job.

When she didn't get it, Linda boiled. Being bypassed for the big job made her mad.

One night a tornado fell from an amber sky. Linda ran and cowered behind the desk in the back of the store. She had never heard anything so terrifying in all her life. When the twister hit, it took out plaza walls as if they were cork. Two places down a guy was killed in the pet store, smothered when the roof smashed the back-room desk he had taken shelter under.

That night, late, on her way home, Linda saw, almost as if for the first time, the dark shapes of the hills north of the city outlined like a shroud over the backdrop sky of a million stars. She drove slowly and smelled sweet grass. And when her father met her at the door, she hugged him tighter than she had in years.

People who've looked death straight in the eye often learn best how to live. Plane crash victims will tell you as much; so will people who are terminally ill. They learn to be content.

No one knows much about Agur, but his prayer teaches all of us something about life: to be content is really a blessing because daily bread—no more, no less—helps us focus on God.

Thank you for so many blessings, Lord. Keep us content. Forgive us when we spend our energy wanting more. In your name, Amen.

CHOICES III

Nancy

I don't know exactly why I quit dating Chad . . . Well, maybe I do. There was something about him I didn't trust.

It had nothing to do with other girls or anything—not at all. I think in his own way he really liked me. In fact, I know he did. He hated breaking up. When I told him we were through, his temper got way out of hand. It scared me. But that wasn't the reason I broke up with him.

It was other things—like the time we were at the ski lodge with all his friends. Chad's so rich it's almost a problem. Everything's got to be perfect all the time—the right boots, the right skis. You wouldn't believe how much he paid for a stocking cap.

So we're sitting there drinking hot chocolate, and he's waving to all his good buddies, rich kids like he is, and he's wearing this party smile. I don't know—Chad is really nice, but it seems somehow that you never know what he's really like. He's so hot, and he dresses perfectly, but it's like there's stuffing underneath all those great clothes. I got the feeling sometimes that he didn't really care about me—only about being seen with me.

So we're sitting there, and he's complaining that his skis didn't really perform. "Five hundred bucks," he says, "I can't believe it. They didn't respond. I could have been on two-by-fours."

Then he looks at me. He looks me straight in the face, but kind of avoids my eyes. And he says to me, right out of nowhere, "Nance, take that barrette out of your hair. It looks better when it's down." He's talking about his worthless five-hundred-dollar skis, and just out of nowhere he tells me to change my hair. I mean, he's my date, not my fashion consultant.

If he would have sworn at me, it wouldn't have made me as mad as that comment did. I knew right then that he was taking me out not because I was a nice person but because I looked good on him, like a Polo shirt. "Take that barrette out of your hair," he says, telling me how to look. Imagine! It wasn't the first time he'd said something like that, but it certainly was the last time. He made me feel like a hairstyle—you know what I mean?

With Chad I always had the feeling I was pretty, and that's a nice feeling. He's like everybody's dream date. He's got everything—looks, bucks, charm. So I guess he makes you look good too. That's a nice feeling, but it's really only skin deep. I guess I got tired of it. That's why I quit. Chad's skin deep.

I never imagined he'd be at the play. I only know it felt good to be with Gregg. When we passed Chad and Ginny, I felt that Gregg and I were driving off into the sunset—you know, like in a movie, leaving bad stuff in the past.

Poor Gregg. He didn't know any of this. He just asked me out, that's all. And he wound up right in the middle of the war.

Sometimes we know very well what's right and wrong, but we seem unable to take the right road. We all need to be stronger, Lord, to fight back the urge to make ourselves look good, for whatever reason. Forgive us for our pride, Lord. Amen.

BAD HABITS

Some patterns of living are just plain foolish. Laziness, gluttony, drunkenness, greed—all these ways carry the seeds of self-destruction.

The Proverbs in this set talk about those bad habits. They get pretty graphic—"As vinegar to the teeth and smoke to the eyes, so is the sluggard to those who send him" (10:26)—and sarcastic—when you eat with the king it's better to ". . . put a knife to your throat if you are given to gluttony" (23:2).

The common way to be a fool is to waste and misuse the life God has given you.

THE BEST YEARS

....
Proverbs 6:6-11

Tricia captained the cheerleading squad when she was a senior. At homecoming she made the queen's court, and she set spikers on the volleyball team so well that Coach called her "magic fingers." Even in January she never lost the perfect tan she picked up lifeguarding at the pool, and most weekends she could have had a half-dozen other dates if she hadn't stuck with Mark.

After Tricia graduated, she worked as a check-out clerk at Ted's and took a night class in sociology at the community college; but books were never her thing. She married Mark when she was nineteen, had two kids, and kept working—stocking shelves and ringing up customers when she wasn't making meals and chasing her kids.

Last night Rita, Tricia's little sister who's starting high school this fall, baby-sat the kids. Tricia split a Diet Coke with her when she got home. "Believe me, Rita," she said, "your high school years are the best years of your life."

Maybe you've heard someone say that. Maybe you've told kids that yourself. Maybe you think it's true.

For some people the high school years *are* the best, I suppose. My guess is, however, that most of those who think that way tend to be Tricia's age or maybe a few years older—probably twenty-something. They're young adults who are busing tables, assembling gizmos in a factory, milking cows, or changing diapers. For them, high school's days of ease seem like only yesterday, and they can't help comparing them to the drudgery of work.

Ever since Adam and Eve took the plunge, work has been our lot in life. But before they bit the apple, our first parents didn't just lie around soaking up all-over tans. Adam and Eve were the first licensed animal scientists—the ones who named aardvarks and zebras. Right from the start, God told the two of them to rule his world.

But with sin came sweat. While sweat cools the body, it appears only with exertion. Sadly enough, work is not always fun, and if that comes as news to you, you're downright strange. We can all be lazy. It's summer now, mid-July, and I can weep just thinking of having to teach again in September. My son would rather steer Mario through a Nintendo maze than sweep the front porch. My daughter would rather leave her clothes on the bedroom floor than pick the place up. My wife would rather eat supper than make it. We're all human. I'd rather water ski than finish this little meditation.

What's more, I resent today's passage because I don't like being compared to no-mind ants. Okay, so they're industrious, but they don't know any better. I'm no ant, and neither are you.

But it's still sad to hear Tricia say her high school years were the best years of her life. Work doesn't have to be a curse. What she told Rita doesn't say much for Mark and the kids, does it? It's as if everything's been downhill for Tricia since the cheerleading squad.

Laziness is a problem, of course, but it's easier to wrestle with it if you like what you do. Work can be a pain, but it can be a blessing too. If you like what you're doing, the best years don't have to be the ones you've left behind in high school.

There, I'm finished. I think I need a break.

Thank you for our opportunity to work in the world you've given us, Lord. Help us to choose carefully the work we do so that we may be a blessing to your kingdom. Amen.

THE BEST YEARS

ON EATING OUT

....
Proverbs 23:1-3; 6-8; 19-21

When I was a kid our family went out for supper about as often I got new shoes. Going out was a real treat.

Times have changed. Fast food places line our highways and compete for our loyalties. Many of us have more money for Whoppers and fries than we have time to mash potatoes and mix up a meatloaf. People simply eat out more than they did thirty years ago.

Today's passages from Proverbs give us three lessons in eating out. Sometimes this book doesn't sound as much like holy Scripture as it does a Hebrew Amy Vanderbilt! Take the lesson in manners in the first three verses, for example.

If you sit down to eat with somebody you really want to impress, don't snort down the clam chowder, use some grace with the stuffed mushrooms, cut the pasta with your fork, don't stick your straw in the chocolate mousse—and for pity's sake, don't burp. Remember! You're trying to impress someone here, so if you feel the urge to eat like the Ultimate Warrior, the verse says, "put a knife to your throat." Control yourself.

The second set of verses take a different angle. If you're having lunch with somebody "with an evil eye" (the Hebrew says), be wary. Don't get taken. The New International Version of the Bible calls this evil-eyed host "stingy"; the New American Standard calls him "selfish." Just exactly what the Hebrew wise men meant isn't crystal-clear.

What we can say, however, is that this evil-eyed character has a different agenda than merely enjoying your company. Whether he's worried about your choosing Maine lobster instead of a coney dog, or whether he's taking you out just to get a contract out of you, it's obvious you are "doing lunch" not because he likes you but because he likes himself.

The wise man says that once it's over, this kind of lunch creeps back up your gullet like a turbulent ball of stomach acid. Eating lunch out under such circumstances is not at all a good time, either during or after.

Verse 19 takes us in a little different direction when it talks about the heart and addresses the sin of gluttony. Its warning is more general and less a matter of good breeding or street smarts.

People my age tend to go out to dinner a lot, because gluttony is about the only real sin available to them. "Oh," we ask, "so you were at the Stratavarious Club?—how delightful! And how did you find the pâté?" (No, "pâté" is *not* French for "the restroom.") "Excellent," we tell each other, "maybe a tad too much oregano."

It's not just the Fatty Arbuckles who sin in the gluttonous mode, says verse 21. Too much eating, like too much drinking, brings drowsiness, a species of laziness. And the path to ruin, financial at least, say the wise men, is littered with lazy bums.

It may be true that "you are what you eat." But Proverbs adds a little to this saying: "You are both what you eat and how you eat it."

Chew on that for awhile.

We sometimes get the feeling that faith is limited to church, Lord—that what we do and say and even eat has nothing to do with being a Christian. Help us to make so strong a commitment that it affects everything we do or say—even how and what we eat. In Jesus' name, Amen.

ROBERT'S DAY

Proverbs 23:29-35

The oaks in Robert Mander's neighborhood tower over the old brick estates, throwing graceful shadows over homes people see as the great American dream. Robert drives his Saab into the city every morning—a half-hour ride from porch to parking stall. Robert's son just received a Rotary club scholarship for four years of leadership at Windrose High, and his daughter is in law school. He's worked in the city office for ten years as a clerk in budgeting. Robert is a CPA, an elder in the church, and a drunk.

Beneath the drivers' seat lies a bottle of vodka he sips from on the commute downtown while thinking over his plans for the day. His office has been remodeled now, and his desk is in a complex of dividers—six-foot walls so short he doesn't dare to risk a drink in his chair. He's got to figure out alternatives.

As he exits the freeway, Robert remembers what he still has stashed in the restroom and guesses he can get by on what's left for another day. But he'll need another bottle in a day or so, especially if he visits the restroom more than three times.

On the sidewalk downtown, Robert figures out lunch. He can get a couple martinis from the bistro just down the block—or, if he has to, he can grab a sandwich and hike back up to the car. For afternoon coffee, he can lock himself in the elevator long enough to get another swig, and, if he needs to get something late in the afternoon, he can always tell his secretary he's got to go to parks and management for some additional figures on next year's budget. He tries to remember what's still in his desk.

As Robert opens the office building door, he tells himself he'll have to stop for another bottle on the way home—at that place with the drive-in window on Halifax. He wonders how much cash he has, but then remembers that he can always drop his card in the Wizard machine behind the bank and pick up a few extra bucks.

"Good morning," his secretary says when she sees him come in. "Grigsby called. He wants you at a meeting right away at nine—long-range planning. Figure on all morning, he said."

Robert scowls.

"Your schedule says you're free," she tells him. "Did I forget something?"

"No," he says, and he swings into his office space.

A committee meeting will throw off the whole day. He'll have to change plans, visit the john earlier, or else get himself in the elevator right away. Stupid meetings, he tells himself. He opens the bottom drawer of his desk, shoves the folders up from the back, and curses to himself when he sees there's no more than four good swallows of treasure left . . .

Robert is no street drunk, but he drinks too much. Getting his booze has become the major concern of each day of his life.

If Proverbs is right in crystal-balling his path in the next months and years, the life and times of Robert Mander will only get worse. Committee meetings, family, church—nothing really matters to him. The moment he gets up in the morning all he really cares about is getting another drink—and another, and another, and another, and another. Not wise, says Proverbs.

....

*We don't know much about alcoholism, Lord, but we
do know that it hurts everyone involved with it.
Forgive us when we fall into our own way
of dealing with difficulties, even everyday events.
Keep our trust in your way strong. Help us
to deal with our lives in ways that bring
praise to your name. Amen.*

GREED

....

Proverbs 23:4-5; 30:15-16

Drugs aren't really evil. Marijuana can be a blessing to cancer patients, heroin has kept people out of a lot of pain, and Coca-Cola, remember, got its name from cocaine. Very little in God's world is pure, unadulterated evil.

Money—what we use to buy what we need—isn't all evil either. Money itself isn't sin.

But the love of money is. In fact, as the New Testament says, the love of money is the root of all evil. Everybody likes money, I suppose, but when we start turning ourselves inside out to feed our own appetites for it, we're guilty of greed.

Someplace, somewhere, in the dim light from a single candle, there's a skinny old woman with steel-wool hair who's sticking a wad of crumpled dollar bills into a patched gray sock, all the while mutteringly madly to herself. Once she's finished, she glances quickly out her window, lifts her mattress, and lays the treasure down. Then she goes to her cupboard and gets out a can of dog food, opens it, and starts to spoon it gleefully into her mouth. One day she'll leave her fortune to her cat.

We all recognize her. She's greedy, she's nuts, and she's an easy way out for us: as long as we hang the word *greed* on weirdos and comic-book characters, we're clean ourselves. It's the miserly wacko who's greedy—not us.

In the Middle Ages, people thought a toad was a perfect symbol of greed. They believed that while toads loved to eat dirt, they wouldn't, fearing that sometime, sooner or later, they'd run out. Greed knows there's never enough.

I have no friends who are toads, so I'm not sure about the accuracy of the theory. But the idea is fitting. Greed is, like the grave (our passage says), never really satisfied—even though it's always eating. How many of us think we have enough money? Most of us wouldn't think of calling ourselves rich—even though we have our butts in the butter when compared to starving Ethiopians. Greed's appetite is never satisfied, even though he eats like a tapeworm.

The Bible's best story about the use of money is the parable of the good Samaritan. Some yokel falls among thieves who kick him, rob him, and leave him for trash. Two really important religious types pass him on their way to a board meeting. Then, a scrubby Samaritan picks him out of the ditch, gets him help, and slaps down a blank check to cover the bills.

If you want to know how to spend money, read about the good Samaritan. There's not an ounce of greed in the man. To him, the money isn't important—except as a means to help other people.

Sooner or later, money, says the wise man, sprouts wings. It accelerates in an eagle's perfect silence, and it's gone.

John Milton claims the angel named Mammon never looked up to God when he walked in heaven; instead, his eyes were constantly cast down on the streets of gold. That's why he was dumped out into hell with his buddy Satan.

Greed. It comes naturally to those who take their eyes off God.

The gift you've given us, the gift of life and even eternal life with you, is the greatest gift we will ever receive, Lord. And it was given freely. Help us to understand that your gift is the pattern for our giving. Help us to give, and keep us from greed. Amen.

CHOICES IV

Chad

The way I figured, if I could talk to her for five minutes, she'd understand. If I could explain to her that I was sorry for what I'd said when we broke up, if I could tell her it wasn't *me* saying those things because I'm really not a bad guy, everything would be fine.

I stuck a tape in and cranked it up. Ginny wasn't saying much after what I'd said about her getting out of the car. She just sat over there in the Arctic circle, looking straight ahead at the road.

So I headed toward Mariah's. It's really the only place special to go in this dinky town when you're all duded up. That's why I went there. I never thought of *them* being there. I admit I knew Nancy and Gregg were going to the play, but the only reason I took Ginny to Mariah's was because it was the nicest place in town to go. Honest.

When we stopped at a red light, I turned down the volume. "Hey," I said, "I'm sorry. You speaking to me yet or not?"

Ginny wasn't crying or nothing, just acting wounded—you know that thing girls do. "For what?" she said.

"For being a jerk," I said, and right away she smiled. "I get carried away sometimes," I admitted.

By that time we were almost at Mariah's. I took a right off Hancock and headed in. The place was full, cars all over, and I started thinking about waiting in line— which is not my favorite thing to do, especially if I'm not with Nancy.

I didn't hit their car on purpose. I swear it. I was just taking my good-natured time looking for a spot, getting hungry and everything, and just like that this Gregg backs up. Any idiot could have parked that car without having to back up. I'm thinking the guy must have bought his license.

I saw them, but out of the corner of my eye. And Ginny screamed— she shouldn't have done that. She yelled "Look out" right in my ear. After that I couldn't help it. I really couldn't. What'd he want me to do, veer over to the other side and whack somebody else's car? I mean, it was all that geek's fault. He backed up, and I couldn't miss him.

Then came the shrieking sound of metal on metal, and I heard my plastic fender pop like a balloon. I mean, a guy's hardly responsible for what happens when he steps outside his car and sees it mashed like that just because of some dork who doesn't know how to park his old man's car, you know? Like I say, I was thinking it's not my fault. No way.

So I got out mad, slammed the door, I guess—I don't remember everything. I took one look at my car, and I lost it. But, cripes' sake, it wasn't my fault. He shouldn't have backed up. He was into my space. Honest to God. You can't blame me.

That's exactly what I was thinking.

Forgive us for forgiving ourselves when we shouldn't, for avoiding blame and deliberately hurting others when we think only of ourselves. Help us to see ourselves clearly and to love others as we would be loved ourselves. Amen.

WICKED OR RIGHTEOUS?

Proverbs mentions two categories of people—the wicked and the righteous, otherwise known as the foolish and the wise.

The wicked delight in evil; ". . . their feet rush into sin, they are swift to shed blood" (1:16). They are full of pride and envy. Eventually, ". . . the unfaithful are destroyed by their duplicity" (11:3).

The righteous delight in what is good and pure. Humble in words and acts, gentle in dealings with others, generous in sharing all good things, in the end ". . . the righteousness of the upright delivers them" (11:6).

THE CROOKED AND THE STRAIGHT

....

Proverbs 10:20-32

I don't know about you, but one thing about the Old Testament that really bugs me sometimes is how much emphasis it places on being righteous. *Righteousness*, the Proverbs and other Old Testament books seem to say, involves being a model human being.

I don't *want* to be a model human being. Nobody does. A model is nothing more than a mannequin—not human at all. I certainly don't want other people to think of me that way. In fact, if you'd say, "The man that writes these devotionals must really be a righteous guy," I don't think I'd take it as a compliment.

I'm not so sure I want to be righteous. Maybe being an all-around good guy is okay, but righteous? Sounds stuffy. Makes me a scowler, someone who looks like skin just out of the bathtub.

Righteous people don't let their kids read *The Hobbit* because they think Satan is lurking behind some soot-edged cloud on the Misty Mountains. Righteous people are scared stiff of bookstores and movie theaters. Righteous people sit home at night and read the Bible—but not all the stories. Righteous people are prudes. Their favorite song is "Be careful little eyes what you see." Righteous people like to tell me what I should be. I guess being righteous today is really a bad rap.

So I don't want to be called righteous—not only because of the bad rap but because the description doesn't fit: If being righteous means being perfect, I'm a long way from it.

But maybe that *isn't* what righteousness is all about. When I read these Proverbs closely, I pick up a little different picture. Verses 20-24 and 31-32, for instance, explain that righteous people are wise—they do the right thing by knowing when to say what's right. When they talk to other people, what they say is "choice silver" that "nourishes many" and "is fitting." Being righteous, according to the passage, is not snooping through other people's trash, but simply knowing when to say the right thing. That's not so bad.

The other Proverbs in the passage are almost like promises. The righteous will find their desires granted, will "stand firm forever," will live a long time, and will find refuge in the way of the Lord. I especially like verse 28: "The prospect of the righteous is joy, but the hopes of the wicked come to nothing." Joy isn't hard to like. As people say about getting old, it's a whole lot better than the alternative.

Sometimes Christians give themselves a bad name; they make righteousness seem like a straight-jacket. What the Proverbs say is that the righteous man is prudent, the righteous woman wise. They know when to speak and when to hold their tongue. And when they talk, what they say is just right.

If you follow the history of the word *right* far enough back, you'll end up in the vicinity of the word *straight*. Something may have changed in what righteous means today, but consider the alternative. I may not jump for joy if you call me righteous, but I'd rather have you think of me as straight than crooked.

To me, *straight* means "honest"—and you can call me that anytime.

Lord, help us to be righteous, even if we don't always like what that word seems to mean. Help us be clean without being uptight, straight without being arrogant. Help us to love you and do your work in the world honestly. Amen.

PRIDE

....
Proverbs 16:5, 18-19

Gluttony turns people into blimps. Greed makes us so hungry for bucks that we're consumed by our appetites. Lust doesn't give a hoot about anybody else as long as it satisfies itself. Laziness would file a claim as King of the Couch Potatoes if he didn't have to get off his posterior to fill out the form. Wrath turns us into clenched fists, explodes out of us in words we draw from the rotten muck of our souls. Envy—well, we'll get to that one later this week. But pride—of all the seven deadlies—pride is the alpha and the omega of sin.

Why? Because pride is the linchpin. We eat and drink too much because we put our appetite before our reason. We're greedy because we think we deserve better than what we got. We lust because we think we're worth the goodies we ogle. We're lazy because we think work is beneath us. We get mad when somebody cuts a hole in our dignity. And we envy because we can't stand the thought of some yokel having it better than we do.

The six other deadly sins—envy, wrath, lust, laziness, greed, and gluttony—are the graceless kids of godfather Pride. So when the Proverbs talk about pride, they're at the very heart of sin itself: when we're proud, we simply elevate ourselves above God.

Sometimes pride is very easy to spot: a gunner, a one-man team, the fancy-pants pole-vaulter who takes all day to make his approach because his hair gets messed in the wind, the swelled-head student who flashes her A like a billboard. At other times pride hides deceptively behind something like taste: "Do you believe that shirt Zimbo is wearing? Talk about horror!"

Just as ugly—and even more sinful—is the kind of spiritual pride typical of many of the characters in the stories of the Christian writer Flannery O'Connor: "Felix calls himself a Christian, but I saw him gobble a Big Mac, even though they're packaged in that horrible unregenerate styrofoam."

Is it wrong to be proud of what you do? You fix up a '57 Chev—work hard for a year, giving everything a spit-shine. Are you grandstanding if you drive it around? Is it wrong for me to think that some story I write really is good? Can't I be proud of tooting my clarinet and not making one minuscule mistake? I aced my final—is it wrong for me feel good?

The answer to all of the above is, of course, no. People who feel like worms often have trouble looking up from their own wretchedness. Take the wind out of someone's sails, and they'll stand in dead water. It's not a sin to take pride in what you're doing.

A deep theologian once lectured at a country church. One listener claimed she missed some fine points: "I didn't understand a word he said," she confessed, "but I know he made God great."

That's the point, I guess.

If you make God great through what you are or what you've done or what you're about to accomplish—if you really do, in your heart, not just with your lips—then go ahead and cruise in that '57 Chev.

But it's tough, isn't it? Sure it is.

There's no one we'd rather have on top than our-
selves, Lord. Keep us from being proud, from stand-
ing like Pharisees and looking down on other people.
Keep us on our knees before your face. Amen.

ENVY, GLOATING, AND JEALOUSY

....
Proverbs 14:30; 24:1-2; 27:4

In Milton's *Paradise Lost*, God Almighty sweeps the rebel Satan and all his buddies out of heaven. They tumble like winged starlings into hell, but they don't throw in the towel. Down there, afloat on the lake of fire, Satan pulls himself up by his bootstraps. He delivers a pep talk good enough to win him a coaching job anywhere in the NFL, telling his singed friends to pick up their chins: he'd rather be king in hell, he says, than a cursed slave in heaven.

Satan's speech may be the most famous lines of the book, a real burst of eloquence. Lots of Milton's readers love it so much that they think of Satan as the book's real hero. After all, he stands up to the tyrant who threw him out.

Satan's sin—at least in heaven—is pride, and the point here is that pride sometimes looks marvelous, God-like. When a kid has her act together—when she knows what she wants and she's tough enough to go for it—we can't help but envy her, even if she's really arrogant.

It's an odd thing, but envy—a sin considered second-fiddle only to pride—is exactly the opposite. An old Latin proverb says that he who envies another admits his own inferiority. Pride is an orator; envy grumbles. Pride bats cleanup; envy sulks at the end of the bench. Pride solos; envy whines.

As always, the Proverbs mince no words. Don't envy other people, they tell us, and they give two good reasons: first, your body will rot, and second, the ones you envy—the rich and powerful—usually end up losers.

Strangely enough, envy is popular among winners: "I got all A's last year except for a B+ in geometry—a class I just hated. Wouldn't you know it?—Candy-butt Andy got all A's. He's such a puke."

Envy bothers real losers, too, of course, but it's a true parasite in those who almost win. It's jealousy of the worst kind.

Envy's flip-side is gloating: "Did you ever see Andy try to handle a puck? He's a pure clutz. Putting skates on him is a criminal act. He gets on the ice and people take cover." Gloating makes us feel like winners when the real winners lose.

Envy, quite simply, whines about the other guy's success and cheers at his failure. Is it common? You bet it is. I'm guilty of it, and—my bet is—so are you.

An odd thing happens to Satan in *Paradise Lost*. The strapping hero becomes a slithering reptile. The more jealous he gets of God, the uglier he becomes: first a snake, then a toad.

Envy rots the bones, says Proverbs. It turns us into toads in basement worlds of our own.

"My brother gets to go to Great America—it's not fair."

"My sister's been water-skiing all afternoon—while I've been doing the lawn."

"If I can't go, then neither should you."

It'll get you. "Anger is cruel and fury overwhelming," says Proverbs, "but who can stand before jealousy?"

Forgive us for wanting what others have, Lord, whether it's money or clothes or the ability to play ball. We can't thank you enough for loving us, even when we don't deserve it. Thank you, Jesus. Amen.

WHY WORK?

....

Proverbs 11:24-27; 25:21-22

You're going to hate me for this. In fact, once I get it all down, I may be sorry for saying it. But here's my beef.

The idea that part-time jobs are good for teenagers is just plain hooey. Recent studies have suggested that kids who work part time have problems with alcohol and drugs, perform poorly in school, and pick up awful attitudes toward work itself.

The conventional wisdom here, is, of course, that learning to punch a time clock is a solid education in that prestigious institution, the school of hard knocks. If a sixteen-year-old learns good work habits flipping burgers, she's on her way.

It doesn't happen. Just about every study done in the last decade proves EXACTLY the opposite. Yet, two-thirds of all eleventh and twelfth graders in North America—and half of all tenth graders—hold down jobs during the school year. That's a crime.

Okay, I have a vested interest. Every semester I see kids who've just graduated from high school, kids who write sentences like these: "Okay, so educashun today doesn't work. Why don't we fixit? If we can stick a man on the moon." College kids.

When kids work twenty hours a week—even if the jobs they do are no more stimulating than bagging groceries or busing tables—it's hard for them to sweat much about Wordsworth, Napoleon, or geothermal energy. The United States is the only industrialized nation in the world where kids are encouraged to take part-time jobs while they are in high school. Is it any wonder that U.S. high school students fall in academic performance year after year?

Okay, but if what those kids earned is being invested or spent wisely, their work has lasting benefits, right? Sure, but it's not. Studies prove beyond a shadow of a doubt that most kids spend their minimum wages on cars, T-shirts, Walkmans, and, too often, drugs and booze.

If kids learn that work is what you do to buy accessories, they're learning sin, and they're off on a mad rush to self-indulgence. "In a consumer society [like ours]," says Ivan Illich, "there are inevitably two kinds of slaves: the prisoners of addiction and the prisoners of envy." Part-time work during the school year transforms kids into consumer slaves. I'm not making this up.

But what has this tirade to do with Proverbs, you ask? Easy. Ask yourself why work is important. Because it takes care of business, right?—food on the table, clothes on your back. The real reason for work, so obvious in the passages today, is not what the money we earn does for us, but rather what it does for others. We earn it to give it.

Lunacy, right? Listen to Proverbs: "A generous man will prosper; he who refreshes others will himself be refreshed." It's better to give than to get.

If your job is keeping you from what's important, it's one thing; but if it's teaching you to hoard, then it's teaching you to sin—whether you're sixteen or sixty.

If you're generous, the Proverbs say, you're blessed. That's what work is all about.

And I'm not sorry I said it either.

....

If we could only begin to love others at all costs as
you have loved us, we could learn to be happy.
Strengthen us to do the right thing, Lord. Build in
us a mind that's like yours. Amen.

CHOICES V

Sam Woolridge

My wife and I were coming out of Mariah's, where we'd just had dinner. We've been separated, and this was the first time we'd been together in weeks. She wanted to try again, but the evening hadn't been very promising. Maybe it was my fault.

Like I told the cops, I didn't see it happen. I heard the crash—we both did—but we didn't see it. I was just opening the restaurant door, and I wasn't looking for trouble. But I heard it. You couldn't *not* hear it. All accidents sound alike—some are just louder.

By the time we got out there, the kid from the Mustang had popped the boy in the Lincoln—I don't know their names. The door of the Mustang was still leaning open, music flooding out, and the driver of the Lincoln was leaning up against the back fender with his wrist up to his lips. Blood too.

I didn't want to get involved, but Ann said, "Don't you think you ought to go over there?"

The Mustang was bashed. In the lights, the shards of glass glistened like broken pieces of a mirror. And it looked like the Lincoln's fault—halfway out of his space like that.

So maybe the guy driving the Mustang had a right to be mad, but he didn't have to be so cocky. He's the kind of person who just can't leave well enough alone. Don't ask me what he said exactly, but it wasn't pretty. Big show-off-type kid. And then he swung again. Not for any good reason, really. The other guy wasn't egging him on.

I know what it's like to just blow out like that—that's one of the things that caused trouble in our marriage. So I went over and grabbed that cocky kid, took him around the shoulders with my arms. But I no more than had his hands up and he slipped away and turned on me. I'm not sure exactly what happened after that, but I think this is the way it went: He swung, and I caught it with my arm. Then the girl yelled. I hadn't seen her before. "Look out!" she said—and like a dummy I turned. That's when he nailed me.

I don't like being blindsided, especially not by some arrogant kid. So I swung, and I hit him—not hard enough to put him out or anything, just hard enough to knock some sense into him. But maybe I shouldn't have . . . . What is he, sixteen?

He staggered back and grabbed his face. Then he looked around as if all of a sudden he'd seen the light. He looked at me and at the other guy and at the girl who had her face in her hands, standing over on the other side of the Lincoln.

Then he took off. I remember noticing how he almost forgot the girl he was with. He limped around to the door of the Mustang and, if she hadn't chased along and yelled, he would have left without her. I never thought of reading the license—it's funny how your mind works. All I could think about was how awful it looked for him to leave without even thinking of her. He didn't care. She did—that was obvious.

And then Ann was at my elbow. "It seems like I've seen this before," she said.

She has. I shouldn't have swung, should I?

....

All of the prayers in the world won't work if we
don't try to reflect your love for us. You've promised
to be our God if we will be your people. Help us to be
your people. Amen.

CHOOSING FRIENDS

Proverbs deals with social realities. We may have the best of characters—good, gentle, kind-hearted. Even so, violent, angry, and lustful friends can corrupt us. The temptation of certain people, certain places, and certain ways can prove virtually irresistible. "Bad company corrupts good character" (1 Cor. 15:33).

The wise person chooses friends who are good-hearted, even-tempered, considerate, and helpful. "He who walks with the wise grows wise, but a companion of fools suffers harm" (13:20).

THE DAYS OF THE HARLEYS

....
Proverbs 1:10-19

When I was little, my older sister sometimes hung around with guys she thought to be more desirable than my parents did. I thought they were cool—tough-looking hombres in rolled-up shirt-sleeves who wore their long hair in the kind of tangled mess you get from an afternoon of tooling around on a Harley-Davidson.

I'm not sure any parents like seeing their kids straddling motorcycles, but it wasn't the Harleys that made my parents wince and stutter when my sister's way of choosing dates came up around the supper table. It was the faith of those boys—or rather the lack of it. In short, my parents didn't approve of the hunks in the driveway.

My sister was no dummy. Instead of caving in to my parents' disapproval, she used the Great Commission to defend herself: go into all the world and preach the gospel. She claimed the guys whose engines rumbled menacingly in our driveway were searching for something in their lives—some meaning she claimed she could give them. "They're good guys," she'd say, "but they're mixed up, and I'm helping them."

Even my dad was at a loss for words.

I was young enough to believe her, but he, I know, didn't.

My sister's defense was the old "salt argument." She claimed that Christians are the salt of the earth, that we have to work as a preservative—or at least something like that. It was all there—right in the Scriptures, she said.

My parents weren't sure that salt was the relevant item from the shopping list. They were thinking of apples—rotten ones. A rotten apple, they claimed, could spoil not only the one next to it but the whole bushel.

As it turned out, my sister didn't marry one of the Harley hunks. She fell in love with a guy she met at college, and as far as I know, there's no Harley in their garage. I'm not sure what's happened to those guys who used to set cups tinkling in the kitchen cupboard with one heavy kick-start out front of our house. Who knows but that my sister *did* do some good in their lives?

The advice of the parents in Proverbs 1 sounds very like my parents' fears in those tricky discussions I used to sit in on years ago. Of course, the parents in Proverbs knew exactly what that gang of toughs was up to—they were hoodlums, all right, plain and simple. My parents didn't *know* my sister's dates were hoods. They simply looked the part—and they weren't Christians.

I've still got some sympathy for my sister's argument, just as I have some sympathy for Ginny, in the story we're reading once a week. Chad is starting to look more and more like a real jerk to me, but Ginny said long ago that she was going to stick with him because he was her friend. I like that. I like Ginny.

What we all need is the ability to tell a bully from a buddy, to know what builds us up and what tears us down. The warning of Proverbs 1 is really very simple: stay away from sin, and violence is a dead end. My sister would agree, both today—and even way back in the days of the Harleys.

You've given us the command to go into the world and preach the gospel, Lord. Help us do that well— whether we're in some far-off country or parked in the driveway. Thank you for your gospel of love and joy. Amen.

TO BLOW A FUSE

....

Proverbs 15:18; 22:24-25; 29:22

"There is not in nature a thing that makes a man so
deformed, so beastly, as doth intemperate anger."
—John Webster

I don't have to draw a picture of anger; I've got one already—Chad.
Right now he's seething in his precious Mustang, flying down the highway, trying to bathe his wounds.

I told you I like Ginny for hanging in there with him, for risking a lot
to be his friend. But Ginny's just seen a real Hollywood-hideous
monster rise out of her friend, and you can bet she's scared. She's
seen the witch of anger conjure up a beast from her buddy, watched
rage cock his quick fists.

Stay away from people who get hot, says Proverbs, or you'll burn
up just like they do.

A fifteenth-century friar named John Gregory separated the sins
we've been talking about this way: he linked pride, envy, and wrath
and called them "sins of the Devil"; the others—lust, laziness, greed,
and gluttony—he called "sins of the flesh."

Pride separates us from God by bringing him down to second chair
while we take over first. Envy separates us from other people because
we want so badly what they have. Anger, the third of the "sins of the
Devil," separates us from ourselves and makes us monsters. If you've
ever seen someone lose it, you know what anger can turn us into.
Ginny knows. She's seen Chad.

Is it wrong to be angry? Does the Bible say we all have to be girl
scouts all the time? Nope.

King David claimed even God gets angry: "Lord," he says in the psalms, "please don't punish me when you're mad." Christ got upset and angry with people too—with the money-changers in the temple, with rich farmers, with King Herod, with a slob who wasn't dressed right for a wedding, and just about every Pharisee in town: "a generation of snakes," he called them.

In a Sietze Buning poem, an catechism teacher flies off the handle when a kid smarts off by answering a question, "I don't care." The teacher loses it right in church. You can swear at me, he says, but don't ever say "I don't care." That was righteous anger, I think—but then I'm an old teacher myself.

So when is anger wrong? According to Proverbs, when it gets other people mad at each other, when its heat flares up into strife, when it puts the whole school in a fit.

And not all our anger is righteous. What makes us spit, more than anything, is humiliation. Our dignity gets black and blue somehow ("Sherry said you're the one who's lying"; "Kyle took all the guys and left me home"), and we get hot—boy, do we get hot. That kind of petty anger isn't righteous; it's only self-defense. Too often we burn up about our own stubbed egos.

Peace is the virtue across the field from anger, but being peaceful doesn't mean having to be a sweetie-pie or a pushover or a wallflower. Peace is simple; it comes from knowing the Lord.

The fear of the Lord is the beginning of wisdom. That's the whole story of the book of Proverbs. Just this once, let's change the words: The fear of the Lord is the beginning of peace. That's just as true, I'm sure.

Some of us blow up all the time, Lord, and some of us never do—we just hold it in. Help us to control our anger. Help us to keep our wits. Let us go when there's good reason, but restrain us from blowing up about selfish things. Give us loving hearts. Amen.

LUST

....
Proverbs 7:6-23

Any pastor who's preached sermons on the Ten Commandments
will tell you that when good old number seven comes up, the church is
packed and bright-eyed. "Adultery this week," the pastor says, and
everybody snaps to.

Love's shadowy cousin, Lust, is the sweetest of the seven deadly
sins because, like anger, it's really not all bad. If you don't really desire
the person you're about to marry, pull on your Nike Airs and take off.
Love is at least partially desire.

Lust, like love, has its roots in sexuality, and sexuality (to me at
least) isn't easy to talk about. Why? Probably because it's such a
mystery—even to someone as old as I am.

What sex does, of course, is make kids. But that's not all. It satisfies
something in us, some desire to love and be loved intimately. Lust
comes at least partially from the same source.

Desire rises in us from something deep and mysterious, something
we've never really been able to keep a lid on. For years people have
claimed that if we'd just talk more about sex, then unwanted pregnan-
cies, divorce, abortion, and now AIDS would vanish.

But does talk help? You judge. Today just about every movie has a
steamy love scene, sex therapy goes public on talk radio, and I sometimes have to blush when I look at my daughter's *Teen* magazine. Yet,
even in Iowa, the number of unwed mothers has doubled in the last fifteen years. And the AIDS epidemic continues to grow.

The passage from Proverbs that you read today is probably the
longest story in the whole book. A young kid strolls down a sidewalk on
the wrong side of town. A woman meets him, tells him she's ready for
him, that her husband's gone on business. The young kid goes along
with her, "little knowing," the Bible says, "it will cost him his life." Not his
money—his *life*.

Everything in the story is hidden in darkness and whispers. We could make it into a mini-series if only it had a different last line: "It will cost him his life" would not be too popular with most North American viewers.

Yet that's the warning of the story and of so much talk about sex—and even more importantly, deceit—in the book of Proverbs. Follow sin to the inner chambers, and you'll pay with your life.

Lust, not love, sacrifices promises, kids, and even faith simply to feed itself. It rips off what it wants from someone else's dignity. It is hatred in the delightful disguise of love.

Lust, not love, is sin.

Help us to recognize when what we want is something we're ordering only for ourselves, Lord. Help us to see that love never ends with a good-night kiss. Keep us strong and pure and holy. In Jesus' name, Amen.

BE THERE

....
Proverbs 3:27-35

Sometimes I think that if I were to bind the essays, stories, and anecdotes I read every school year, I'd have a book the size of the Chicago yellow pages. Maybe that's an overstatement, but I do read a ton of papers, at least enough to pick up what kids are thinking.

One phrase I stumble over time after time these days is the phrase "be there." It pops off the page. How do you define a friend? Someone who will "be there." I see it so often I've begun to mark it as a cliché. "Be there," the paper says, and I scratch in something like "Be specific," "Be clear," or "What exactly does that mean?"

Actually, I do know what "be there" means—and so did the wise men of the Proverbs. "Being there" means not turning out the lights on a friendship when the kid you've grown up with doesn't make the team and you do. It means talking forever into the night when your friend's parents say they're separating. It means not quitting a pregnant girlfriend.

The series of don'ts in today's passage begins with the admonition to "be there." Verses 27 and 28 claim in no uncertain terms that it's wrong to retreat or run away when you've got the power to "be there" for someone who needs your help.

It sounds so simple, doesn't it? Don't turn your back on somebody who's down or spun out of control on the wrong path. But it's not so easy. If it were, my students wouldn't value "being there" so highly and the Scriptures wouldn't need to command us to stick by those who are down and out.

The next two don'ts (vv. 29 and 30) tell us not to antagonize others. You're on a long vacation, and your sister, who's sleeping, sticks her foot three inches over the line that separates your half of the back seat from hers. You're ornery because the sun's been on your side of the car all afternoon. So you plant your fingers behind the sole of your sister's foot and stretch a rubber band all the way back to the door—zap! Getting her is so right, you tell yourself. She knows the rules. But Proverbs says, "Don't plot harm."

The final don't of the passage warns us against setting up Clint Eastwood types as heros. Just after the Vietnam war, you couldn't buy a war toy; today the market is flooded with them. Rambo movies, it seems, have brought GI Joes back with a vengeance. And Nintendo has introduced a whole new range of violent games created to bash an enemy, to machine gun him into a bloody pulp, or to use some form of the martial arts to reverse the action of his Adam's apple. "Don't choose the ways of violence," Proverbs tells us. "Don't envy Rambo."

The message at the end of today's passage—after the series of don'ts—is the promise of honor to those who live graciously with their neighbors, to those who are committed to "being there." Maybe we need to become more like the Lakota Sioux, whose greatest buffalo hunters were given the honor of bringing back sufficient meat for the needy—the fatherless, the widows, and the hungry. Among these mighty Sioux warriors those who helped the people who really needed it were heroes. Every young warrior wanted that job.

Maybe *we* need some new heroes.

Thank you, Lord, for always being there when we need you. No matter what happens, we're always sure that you'll listen to us. No matter what we do, you have promised to be with us. Amen.

CHOICES VI

Neither of them said a word. Chad drove like a banshee straight out of town until he got to the interstate, leaving the lights of the city behind him, the music pounding.

Ginny pulled on her seat belt. "You're bleeding," she said finally, pulling out a Kleenex. "I can get it," she told him, but he turned away from her and pulled off at the rest stop.

Chad screeched into a parking spot, leaving the car running while he went to the restroom to check on his cut. Ginny turned off the engine, pocketed the keys, and followed him inside. She wasn't about to let him go—not in the shape he was in.

As Chad stalked out of the restroom, an older couple walked in.

"Could you kids tell us if we can get a good meal in this town?" the woman said. She had a clown on her t-shirt beneath her open jacket. Her husband was leaning on his cane. "I know it's late, but some nice place?"

Before Ginny could say a word, Chad bellowed something so ugly the woman grabbed her husband's arm. Chad told them Barrington was an armpit—and he said worse things.

The lady held her fingers to her face as they backed out the door.

"Why'd you do that?" Ginny said. "What possible reason—"

"Get off my back," Chad said, rubbing his wrist across the corner of his lips. "All you can do is harp—"

"Just leave," she said. "Now I understand about Nancy."

He jerked around—mad, she knew, but wounded. "Whaddya mean?" he said. "I don't need her."

"Go on," she told him. "You don't need anybody, do you?"

He kept rubbing his hands. "That's the way you want it, huh?" he said. "Listen, I'm the best thing you got." Then he left, jamming the door open with his forearm.

Ginny watched him bull past the old couple on the sidewalk, run back to the car, and get in, slamming the door. She could forget him, she thought, after what he said. She could give him his blasted keys and let him run. She should.

But the door opened again and he climbed out, got down on his knees, and searched the floor for the keys. Down on his knees, Ginny thought—it was good for him.

She stepped outside. "*I've* got them," she yelled. "They're right here," and she dangled the keys in her fingers.

Chad slammed the door and ran back through the grass. She'd never seen his face so wrenched out of shape before. "I'm not giving them to you," she said. "If you want 'em you're going to have to take them from me." She was scared to death, betting on something she'd swore she'd seen before, something good in him, bigger than this wild anger and his lousy pride.

"Don't make me, Ginny," he said.

"I'm all you got right now," she told him, "and I'm not running away. Neither are you. I'm not going to let you."

"Don't do this," he said.

She held the keys behind her.

He was an inch away from bawling, his hands raised in front of his face, his lips tightened. "Did you see my car?" he said. "Did you see what he did? It's a mess."

"You think that's bad," she said, "you should see yourself."

Lord, as much as we enjoy our friends and need
them, we know that there is no one and nothing like
you. You loved us enough to die for us, and you give
us your love and life for nothing. For that we honor
you with our lives. In your name, Amen.

FAMILY

This set of Proverbs deals with family living—with disciplining children and getting along with a spouse.

Peace seems to be the ideal in these verses. But don't misunderstand this as just a "let me alone" kind of peace. What these Proverbs are referring to is *shalom*—that is, prosperity, health, goodness, and a living together before the face of God.

That same *shalom* is pictured in "the wife of noble character" (31:10-31). This woman has all the best qualities: strength of character, diligence, prudence, and endurance. But above all, she is "a woman who fears the LORD" (31:30).

"ISN'T THAT DARLING?"

Proverbs 13:18, 24; 22:6, 15; 23:13-14

My daughter claims that the kids at a place she once babysat took fiendish pleasure in riding each others' bikes. Even though each child (the oldest was six) had a bike of his own, they deliberately stole each other's, and what resulted—every last time—was great wailing and gnashing of teeth.

Kids can be terrors, of course. They can say things to each other that would make adults bleed. They can be greedy as misers, tease unmercifully, kick, beat, and stomp with the best of bullies. They can turn their backs like bigots when some other kid's hair is the wrong color, when her blouse has the wrong collar, or when his th-speech cometh out in a lithsp. If kids were as innocent as we sometimes make them out to be, middle school wouldn't be the kind of snake pit it often is.

Proverbs isn't exactly sweet on kids: "He who spares the rod hates his son" (3:24), the wise men tell us. And how about this: "Folly is bound up in the heart of a child, but the rod of discipline will drive it far from him (22:15)." Ouch. I can feel the welts.

When I was in fifth grade, we took an all-school picture out on the playground. The boys sat on folding chairs, and the girls stood behind us—very humiliating. So we bent over and started chucking stones at their feet. They squealed.

My friends saw the teacher coming. I don't remember seeing him at all. What I do remember is the way he almost tore my face off with his open hand. Some parents today, I suppose, would sue; but my parents—who never found out about it, by the way—would have simply said I was naughty.

Things have changed. Slapping kids around today just isn't done; in most places it's illegal. When my kids were younger, I sang an old song in late August just to tease them:

School days, school days—
Dear old golden rule-days;
Reading and writing and 'rithmetic,
Taught to the tune of a hickory stick . . .

I had to explain the last line to my son because he had no idea what a hickory stick had to do with going to school.

According to some people today, "Spare the rod, spoil the child" is flat wrong—at school or in the home. Maybe they're right. Maybe Proverbs is simply one of those parts of the Bible that don't really count anymore, an area in which we've grown smarter than Scripture.

I don't think so. I've always thought that ordering a teacher or a parent not to use corporal punishment was wrong. But even more wrong, it seems to me, is frequent use of a hickory stick. You can't beat a child into anything but hostility.

What Proverbs is after, of course, is *discipline*, another form of the word *disciple*. My favorite of these verses is 13:24: "He who spares the rod hates his son, but he who loves him is careful to discipline him."

Note the word *careful*. There's no license in that verse to whup the daylights out of any kid. What it says is not so much a promise as a statement of fact: a good mother doesn't smile at her kid's sneer; a good father doesn't back down from a kid's back talk; and a good kid listens.

Love, Proverbs says, means discipline. It's just that simple.

We don't like punishment, Lord, no matter where it comes from. Spare us from punishment, Lord, but make us good and strong and loving members of your family. That's what we want the most. In Jesus' name, Amen.

WAR AND PEACE

Proverbs 15:17; 17:1; 21:9, 19; 27:15-16

It was so hot and thick on Saturday that after a few rounds with the lawn mower, sweat spread over my T-shirt like the shadows of a great plague fallen over the land. After a good start, I hiked to the gas station, because I knew the tank was empty. I put two gallons in the can, then walked inside.

"The wife gotcha' mowin' the lawn?" the kid behind the counter asked.

I didn't know what to say. I just stood there and laughed at the picture he drew with that line. Here's the way he saw it, I'm sure: me, sprawled on the couch slurping a root beer and watching the Cubs on WGN; my wife, her hair full of curlers, yapping at me like a lap dog. "You blamed fool," she says. "Whyn't you get out there and work for a change? The grass is so long that Florentine can't even find her trike." She raises her rolling pin over my head. "I can't believe I ever hitched up to such a lousy bum."

Now I'll grant you that somewhere on God's green earth there likely is a passel of couch potato husbands and a whole coven of witchy wives. If there wasn't, Old Milwaukee wouldn't end every commercial with the same line: a bunch of men—no women—sitting around a campfire, drinking beer and telling each other that "it just doesn't get any better than this."

It's not that way at our place. But then again, nobody's perfect—and nobody's marriage is perfect either. And I'm not about to claim that my wife and I don't have our differences. We do. And when we do, we have decidedly different ways of dealing with them.

Like the image the gas station attendant had, the pictures of the women in some of these Proverbs ("Better to live on a corner of the roof than share a house with a quarrelsome wife") are enough to make me laugh and my wife steam. Of course, if the Proverbs were written for young princesses instead of princes, it's more than likely that what they'd say would make me boil.

It's a dangerous thing to try to make up Scripture, but let's fool around a little. Let's pretend the Proverbs are little chunks of wisdom taught to young, unmarried women. What might they say? How about this: It's better to live alone in the Grand Tetons than to have to put up with a macho man. Or, a husband with an ego problem is a lifetime of migraines.

Don't misunderstand Proverbs. Men, as well as women, can be pains in the neck. The point of all the verses you've read today is that living in peace with a spouse will bring joy; conflict, on the other hand— whether it's from constant quarreling or real abuse—makes life itself torture. "Better a meal of vegetables where there is love than a fattened calf with hatred" (15:17).

When my wife gets angry with me, she steams. When I get mad at her, I boil. We're not alike. But one of the great pleasures of marriage is learning to tune yourself to another's music. It's an art that starts with giving, not griping. And that truth isn't so much mine as it is the Lord's.

For some reason, Lord, it seems that we get the most angry at the people who are closest to us. Keep us at peace with those we love. Enrich our hearts with your Spirit, and help us show your love all hours of the day. Amen.

THE GOOD WIFE I

....
Proverbs 31:10-19

The town where I live sports a newly-paved main street, smooth as a baby's bottom. For a few weeks the acrid smell of blacktop burned our noses, and a quick trip for a loaf of bread meant swerving to avoid the manholes erupting like mini-Devil's Towers from the shaved old surface of the highway. I passed a road grater one day and did an immediate double take. There at the wheel was a person in a hard hat, sleeves cut off, sun-bronzed arms round and thick as hogs' thighs, long scraggly hair matted with dust. What's more, this person was a woman.

Talking about men's roles—and women's—today is like crossing a mine field in that road grater. The wise men of Proverbs would have created quite a stir if they had tried to address the advice in these verses to a group of twentieth-century teenagers!

What exactly do they tell the young princes? In this remarkable, poetic passage that concludes the book of Proverbs, they tell these young men what to look for in a wife.

Poetry began, I'm told, as a way to memorize great stories. Rhyme brings a melody to words that keeps them stuck in your mind. This famous long passage is a poem of a different sort—an alphabetic acrostic: A is for able, B is for beauty—that kind of thing.

No one could really translate that structure into English, so our versions have lost their original poetic form. But what's interesting here is how important this passage must have been. Not only does it come at the end of the book, but it's written so that those who hear it can memorize it forever. According to the wise men, a good wife is pretty important.

What is she like? (Welcome to the danger zone.) She supports her husband, sews a lot, and shops carefully (12, 13, 14). She makes breakfast when the sun is only a glimmer in the east and invests wisely in real estate (15, 16). She's no weakling about her work, knows the market value for her goods, burns the midnight oil, and sews like an expert (17, 18, 19).

Chances are right now there isn't a woman hearing this who isn't either shamed or seething—maybe both. After all, where does it say here that women might spend some time teaching third grade or running a corporate office? We're only halfway through the passage and the picture emerging already sounds like Superwoman.

All right, times change. You don't think so? Then try your hand at making bread. First, grind whole-grain flour and get the yeast a-growin' in potato water, add flour until the mixture gets soupy like a sponge, let it rise for forty-five minutes in a warm oven, add the rest of the flour, punch the tar out of it for a while, let it rise some more, punch it again, grease the pan, punch it again, shape it into loaves, and bake it. Shoot!—forgot the salt? Start over.

Or—get on your mountain bike and buy a loaf at the Piggily Wiggily. Women's work changes. So does men's.

So far, according to the passage, the good wife is diligent, prudent, and caring. Those attributes still create high standards—both for women *and* men. They're really not sexist—just tough.

Bless our marriages, Lord. And bless those of us who still are dating. Make our choices the right ones. Fill us with your grace so we may know your will. Strengthen our families and bring us peace. In your name, Amen.

THE GOOD WIFE II

....
Proverbs 31:19-31

Okay, I give up. Yesterday I said that the passage on the good wife wasn't really sexist. Maybe that's not the whole truth. By contemporary feminist standards, the wise men of the Proverbs are flat-out chauvinist pigs. After all, it's the woman who stays at home and takes care of business while the husband chaws cigars and politics at the city gate. No women are out there in public forum—only men. Okay, it's sexist.

And there's another limitation: the whole passage is aimed at only certain women—rich ones. Purple has been so much the color of royalty through the ages that it's come to symbolize power. Originally, purple dye was extracted in minute quantities from a certain shellfish, making it costly and rare. Only the rich could afford purple robes.

The good wife of Proverbs 31 is clothed in fine linen and purple. It's obvious her husband doesn't carry a lunch bucket to the city gates. We're talking upper echelon here—a woman with servants, real estate, and a husband who's a mover and a shaker. So those of us who don't drive Lincolns don't need to bother with this passage, right? And it's certainly not for middle-class males like me.

Maybe it's not. Let's just pretend for a minute that this passage has nothing to do with life today in the fast lane—the world of AIDS and 2 Live Crew, of the crumbling worlds of communist walls and family ties. Let's just look at it as some historical artifact, a museum tableau of old Hebrew life.

Okay, let's. What does it tell us? Well, verse 20 makes the claim that the Hebrews thought the good, rich woman should care for the poor. Verse 21 claims she's prudent, a provider who's well-prepared and wise (as the Sioux would say, "because she can see beyond the new moon"). Verse 22 says she dresses well.

Verse 23 says her husband is honored downtown—not simply because of who he is either. Verse 24 claims that she's a shark when it comes to the markets, and 25 describes her as a woman of such dignity, provision, and strength that she simply laughs at tomorrow's worries. Verse 26 celebrates her wisdom, her ability to teach right and wrong to her children; 27 honors her industry.

All right. These are the virtues honored by the ancient Hebrews. Aren't they interesting? Write them down and lock them in a museum somewhere, like a delicate clay urn.

Throughout this book we've dealt with each of the seven deadly sins: pride, envy, anger, laziness, lust, greed, and gluttony. The good wife is guilty of none of these. What she shows instead are seven virtues: she's wise, just, courageous in facing life's storms, temperate, has faith in tomorrow, loves her family and her servants, and never lacks hope.

Aren't these ancient values fascinating—worthy of the Smithsonian? Yes. But verse 30 claims they're also the virtues of a woman who fears the Lord. What's more, they're the same virtues that the book of Proverbs praises in a godly man.

Put these verses in a museum if you like, but I much prefer what the wise men say: "Write them on the tablet of your heart."

Sometimes it's easier just to forget what you say in your Word than it is to change our lives. Help us to know your will, Lord, and keep us always humble enough to learn. Amen.

CHOICES VII

Chad

There's not much to do here but watch soap operas. Kids come to visit at night, but during the day it's just me and the nurses and "The Young and the Restless."

You can't be too proud in a hospital. Some things the nurses do for me I'd rather not talk about. But at least I'm here and alive—and I've got lots of days of nothing to do but think.

I couldn't take those keys from Ginny. An angry part of me wanted to, but I couldn't. I don't remember much, but I can still see her standing with her hands behind her, daring me to hit her. She says she knew I wouldn't, but I wouldn't have bet on it myself.

I ran. I took off down the exit ramp and onto the interstate, and the whole time, all I saw was the way Nancy laughed, sitting in the theater beside this guy I didn't know. I heard her. I'm in this awful pain, and she doesn't even care. I'm running down the interstate, and all I hear is her laugh. . .

I'm not angry with her anymore. For a while there I think I considered her as much my property as the Mustang. But I know now that I don't own her and never did.

And I don't hate Gregg. I don't even know him. All of this had nothing to do with him. I think the accident in the parking lot was his fault, but I was crazy for swinging at him the way I did. My hitting him had nothing to do with my car.

How can I be angry with Ginny? More than anybody else in the world, she stuck with me. I'll never forget the look on her face when she hid those keys: scared to death, but absolutely determined. And I knew—even though I couldn't see past the anger burning in front of my eyes—I knew she was right.

So I ran.

Don't tell anyone this because no one knows what really happened. I was running along that interstate, going nowhere, all by myself. The leaves on the trees whispered in the wind, and the sky was dark and starless. I had nothing left, so I veered into the lane. Call it what you want to. Maybe I wanted to die to make people care—I don't know.

The guy saw me in the road and had just enough time to swerve. He hit the brakes and lost it, spun out so that his rear fender slapped me into the ditch like a bug and broke most of the bones in my body. After that I don't remember anything.

Maybe I tried to kill myself, but I couldn't even do that right. Something's been screwy in my life, and I guess I had to wake up here, locked in hospital armor, to see it.

My parents have been here. They're happy I'm alive, but it's different now with them. They seem sad most of the time, blaming themselves for what happened.

Listen. Don't tell anyone about the way I ran into the highway. I've got hours and hours with nothing to do now but think it all through. Sometimes I could just cry.

The therapist is on his way. He makes me flex muscles inside this cast. I tell him that's what I'm doing—and he believes me. But he doesn't know for sure. He can't see inside.

You never know what's really going on inside somebody. Sometimes you don't even know what's going on inside yourself.

....

You are our God, and we are your people, Lord.
Sometimes we leave your side, and sometimes we
come back—but you never leave. You own the world.
Every last inch of it belongs to your rule. Be with us
this day and every day, as you have promised. Amen.

MYSTERIES AND MIRACLES

This last set of meditations reflects on one set of Proverbs, the sayings of Agur, son of Jakeh (chapter 30). Unlike most of the Proverbs, with their contrast of the wicked and the righteous, the ways of wisdom and the paths of folly, these sayings of Agur sound a note of wonder at God's world.

God is great. He deserves our fear and awe. His ways are beyond our comprehension. Truly, "the fear of the LORD is the beginning of wisdom" (9:10).

MYSTERIES

....
Proverbs 30:18-19

I've had enough of caves. Just a week ago, our family took a nearly two-hour hike through Wind Cave in the Black Hills of South Dakota. What we saw was rocks—that's it. They were strewn hither and yon by underwater seas that evaporated, our guide said, a triple zillion years ago. To me, it was two long hours of "boulderdash." (Sorry about that.)

What did interest me was the park ranger telling us how explorers today could still find pages from the 1890s newspapers that people wrapped their lunches when they took long, dark hikes in the cave a century ago. Plain old rocks don't interest me; human beings do.

However, my wife likes caves, and so does my son. So even though I've had my fill of "historic rocks," I expect I'll be talked into viewing a few more. The next time we're on vacation and my family wants to hike through a cave I'll probably go along—even though I'd rather try catching trout on little yellow clumps of Velveeta cheese.

What bugs me is I don't know *why* I don't like caves as much as my wife does. For some strange reason, she likes them—she likes rocks. Strange woman.

Why don't I? Why do they bore me and fascinate her? Maybe when I was a kid I stubbed my toe bad or something—I don't know. It's a mystery.

Sometimes the words of the wise man Agur, which appear near the close of the book of Proverbs, seem as great a mystery to me as why my wife likes rocks and I don't. The passage today even celebrates mystery. Four things, he says, are mysteries to him: the way of an eagle in the sky, the way of a snake on a rock, the way of ship on the high seas, and the way of man with a maiden.

Two strange verses. What on earth do they mean?

Here's one idea. None of the four illustrations follow or leave clearly marked paths. An eagle aloft goes where it will. A snake slithers its own way. There's no road signs on an ocean. And a man with maiden? Well, nobody's love story is exactly like anybody else's. They all have different chapters.

Agur's mysteries are not like the murder mysteries so many of us are drawn to—the type of stories the super-weird Edgar Allan Poe introduced with "The Murders in the Rue Morgue." They are not the whodunits that Sherlock Holmes made a career out of solving and Alfred Hitchcock devoted his life to filming. As anyone who watches "Murder, She Wrote" knows, those kinds of mysteries normally get solved.

In contrast, what fascinates Agur are the things he cannot figure out. What he treasures is pure, unsolvable mystery. He loves what he can't understand, the roads he can't plot and the directions he can't predict. He really gets off on the unexplainable.

I think many of us do.

I don't know why my wife likes caves. But she does. I guess, for whatever reason, she's not exactly like me. In some ways she's a mystery I'll never understand. Maybe that's part of the reason I love her. You figure that out!

*At our very wisest, Lord, there's still things we don't
and won't understand about you and even our
world. Help us to see your hand in everything.
Amen.*

OUT OF ORDER

·······························
Proverbs 30:21-23

A man named Banna Bannadonna (names have been changed to protect the guilty) pulled himself up by his musical bootstraps to become a celebrated organist, leaving behind a raggedy family of pumpkin farmers. Widely celebrated, Bannadonna gave concerts at the finest music halls in London, Frankfurt, and Kalamazoo.

When his own country church decided to spill a little cash on a new pipe organ, they asked young Banna, a son of the congregation, to play the dedication concert, an event sure to draw public radio listeners from around the county.

So Banna packed his bags with Bach, Beethoven, and Brahms, a gala assortment of toccatas and fugues, and made the concert a success. For two hours the valentine blush of bliss on the faces of smartly dressed people glowed beautifully—elegant people leaning politely to each other, nodding at Banna's delicate fingering.

But Banna's father, Oscar, didn't know his son's music. As the crowd stood for the ovation, he felt ornery. Not only did the music seem weird, he couldn't even read the titles. So he stood and put his hands to his face. "How about 'Stars and Stripes Forever,' Benny?" he yelled.

No one said a word, but the little church shook. What Banna's papa yelled was delightfully inappropriate.

This true story carries with it some of the strange texture of this second grouping of illustrations that Agur puts together in the passage for today. For what he talks about here are things that are somehow inappropriate, out of place, even ridiculous, at least to him: a servant leading the nation; a belching bimbo; a loveless marriage; and a sly servant girl who seduces her mistress's husband.

Now it's possible that these examples make Agur sound a little uptight. In North America today, we like to think of someone poor—like a servant—having a shot at becoming President or Prime Minister. It's the kind of thing we celebrate in all kinds of rags-to-riches stories. Agur says it's trouble.

Likewise, a fool full of food. What Agur thinks inappropriate is some airhead getting cocky because he can roam wherever he wants on the buffet line. It's almost better to keep the fools hungry and on their knees, Agur seems to imply. That notion is hardly democratic.

The final two pictures feature marriage. In the first, it seems Agur's intent is to say that a marriage without love is almost certain to bomb—and when it does, there will be destruction. The second is easier: it's awfully inappropriate (and wrong) for a servant girl to chase the master of the house.

To Agur—and the other wise men of the Proverbs, I'm sure— all of these pictures show a world out of joint, people stepping out of line, characters who don't know their place. Agur's sentiments may not be democratic, but behind them lies an ethic which is eternal. In each of the situations he describes, people don't know or don't care what's appropriate for them. To Agur, at least, the earth itself trembles at such chaos.

I still like Oscar's special request to his arrogant son, but Agur warns against the inappropriate. Know yourself and do what's right, he says.

Help us to know our limits, Lord, to not push ourselves beyond what we are or what we can take. Help us to be satisfied with what you've given us, to strive for what we can but to take heart in the fact of your love for us. In Jesus' name, Amen.

GO TO THE ANT

....
Proverbs 30:24-28

- Although a rattlesnake's bite is no picnic, a Black Widow spider's venom is fifteen times deadlier.
- If you scare the daylights out of an elephant, his ears will stand up straight. (Try it next time you see one downtown.)
- Lions will attack humans only from behind. What's more, if you lie on your back, face up, they won't eat you. (You might remember that next time you spend a weekend in Kenya.)
- No matter what you say about jackals, they're smart enough to stay out of divorce court: they mate for life.
- And as long as we're on often-misunderstood villains, how about this: You think a cat is clean? A cockroach spends more time per day cleaning itself up than any slick Siamese.
- If someone says you eat like a horse, tell him he eats like a silkworm. Silkworms gorge ten thousand times their weight every twenty-six days.
- Here's something: weasels and leopards share one sweet trait: they kill for sheer pleasure.

I'm not sure why animal trivia is interesting, but it is. Apparently, Agur must have thought so too. For the last couple of days we've been looking at Agur's strange little quartets: four things he doesn't understand, four things that shake things up, and now four bright little beasts. If you're like me, you're probably starting to wonder what on earth Agur's trivial pursuit is doing in the Bible.

Let's look for clues in today's bestiary.

The first of the midget wiseacres is the ant—absolutely brilliant. Why? Because the ant is smart enough to stick something away for tomorrow. The second, coneys—or rock badgers—are genius-level engineers who sculpt homes out of almost nothing. The third, locusts, don't need bosses because they're diligent and super-organized.

Finally, lizards. This one is a little tough. When I think of lizards, I think of greased lightning in the desert. But the verse claims that these animals are nowhere near as quick as people think: anybody can catch lizards. So, how do these rat-like reptiles fit with Agur's fearsome foursome?

No one is exactly sure, and since Agur's jersey was long ago retired in the wise man's hall of fame, all we can do is guess. We could think of it this way: nobody's dying to get the lizard's job—eating bugs; yet the lowly lizard hangs around with the big shots—on the walls of the king's palace. (Moral: humility works; you don't need to act big-time to get to the top.)

Probably the best-known verse of this entire book is the one that begins "Go to the ant, you sluggard (Prov. 6:6)." Agur carries this advice a little further. As long as you're down at the zoo, he says, check out the badgers, the locusts, and the lizards.

Big smarts, he says, come in small packages. Take heed.

---

*When we're alive to you, Lord, it seems you appear
in the clouds and in the sky, in country landscapes
or in a city's outline against the night. We see you in
the faces of those we love. We even see you in our
sleep. Be with us always, Lord. Keep us safe, but
show us the dimensions of your power in the world
we live in. Amen.*

DON'T SLOUCH

....
Proverbs 30:29-31

Just about everybody gets told not to slouch at least once in their lives. I know I did. My mother and I would be walking along, my shoes shuffling, and she'd say, "Pick up your feet." And because she sang solos, she constantly used to harp at me to hold my head up and sing boldly.

Okay, okay, I harp myself. More than once I've told my son to quit mumbling and speak up.

The last of Agur's little pictures has to do with how we carry ourselves. His pictures are the lesson: the lion, king of beasts; the strutting rooster, lord of the barnyard; a cocky, almost obnoxious, billy goat; and the king with his army.

Stateliness, Agur tells the young princes, should be there in your walk—keep your head up, chin thrust forward, back straight. If you're going to be a leader, don't slouch. Look good. Show some class. Even dress right.

I'm not a particularly good example myself. Here I sit, barefoot, in old shorts and a tank-top, three-days growth of beard on my face. My excuse is that I grew up in the '60s, when only nerds wore new clothes. Back then, we cut off everything except hair—shorts, shirts, shoes—and whenever possible left the fringe. Looking good meant the Salvation Army, not Ralph Lauren.

Maybe my fear of "looking good" was colored by a man named Richard Cory in a poem by Edward Arlington Robinson. Cory, you might remember, looked good—"imperially slim," as I recall. He had everybody's gaze locked up, and yet, one day, he went home quietly and put a bullet through his head.

Agur's little illustrations aren't meant to tell the young princes to show off. What he's drawing their (and our) attention to is dignity— knowing you'll be judged by your appearance. For pete's sake, don't slouch, or you'll be mistaken for one.

* * * * * *

We've spent four days looking at the little riddles of Agur—and not once in these verses have we seen God. So what has this passage—and much of the book—to do with being a Christian?

Remember where we started several weeks ago? "The fear of the LORD is the beginning of wisdom," we learned. That's what this book is all about. Agur's sayings, all the cutsey little phrases, and a hundred-odd Proverbs fit together as a guide for the way to wisdom—and that way starts in the fear of the Lord. Wisdom starts in knowing God.

Wisdom, today, is hardly a hot commodity. In America this year, one million teenagers will get pregnant. Countless others will die in alcohol-related accidents or commit suicide (the suicide rate for teens has doubled since 1968). Still others will get arrested. If you think I'm pointing only at teenagers, remember that they learn everything they know from their parents.

There's silliness galore in our world. Stupidity appears nightly on television screens. Foolishness is epidemic.

You want smarts?—listen! The fear of the Lord is the beginning of wisdom. That's the agenda of the Proverbs—it begins with God, the beginner of all things, the great I AM.

---

*Give us wisdom, Lord, and keep us under the shelter
of your wings. Help us fly with your Spirit, and
make us wise in the power of your will. In Jesus'
name, Amen.*

CHOICES VIII

Ginny

Last week I took Nancy in to see him. I thought if I warned him she was coming, he'd get nervous, so I didn't tell him.

He's so helpless now, wrapped up in that stiff white suit. I kid him, tell him it's a perfect tux. But even though he's confined to that bed, he's as good looking as he ever was. By some miracle the accident that crushed his body never touched his head.

I had to take Nancy's arm when we went in, and the first thing she said was kind of dumb: "How you doin'?" she asked—too cute maybe, as if we're walking down the hallway in school.

There was Chad, hung up in straps and wires—here a leg, there a leg—hadn't moved in two weeks. He smiled. "Everything goes slow," he said. "I got to be waited on. But I'm all right," and he nodded, as if by moving his head he could prove something. "I'm glad you came," he told her. "I got a lot to be sorry for."

When he said that, I had to look away for a minute because I couldn't help remembering the way the Mustang had flown down the interstate, faster than I'd ever gone in my life, him spitting things I'll never repeat to anyone. And now the first thing he told Nancy was that he was sorry—that same Chad. "I got a lot to be sorry for," he told her—almost the first words out of his mouth.

It's really something. You got to be strong to say you're sorry.

When I stood over him that night in the ditch, I asked the Lord to save him, and he did. The rescue squad said right away that Chad wasn't going to die, even though his body was a mess.

But the Lord let somebody die in him. You might even say that the Lord killed somebody in him—the angry Chad, the one so full of pride. Proud people can't say they're sorry like he did, so I guess the Lord answered my prayer. He recognized that more than Chad's life was in danger, and he saved him.

I've always wondered if Chad tried to kill himself. Just today I figured out how to ask him. "Chad," I said, "the driver says you were in his lane."

"Is that right?" he said.

"How come?" I asked.

"Maybe it was dark."

"Sure," I said. "It was late, remember?"

He took a drink from the straw in the glass beside him. "You've got to know everything, Ginny, don't you?" he said. He turned his eyes away from me, staring up at the ceiling.

"I'm not leaving," I told him.

Then he looked back at me. "It was the wrong thing for me to do," he said, "but a funny thing happened. It turned out right. I don't understand, Ginny, but it worked out. I know it was wrong, but it turned out right. It's crazy."

I like sitting beside him. Tons of kids visit him now, and he smiles a lot out of that white cast. Nothing makes him feel better than company.

And it's not so crazy either, I figure. There's only one way to explain what happened: I guess the Lord knew there was more to Chad than what he was that night. I knew it too. Today he's tougher, even though he can't move a muscle. He's healed up, even though he's broken. Crazy.

....

There are times when we don't know exactly how
things are going to work out, Lord. When those
times come, help us to take confidence in what
you've told us in your Word—that things will work
out for those who love you. Thank you for loving us.
Amen.